MW00904609

THE GARGOYLE'S LEFT EAR

The Black Moss Press Settlements series gives writers a creative non-fiction forum for focusing on their roots, the "place" out of which their writing has emerged, and the study of the craft itself.

Books in the Settlements series include:

The Farm On The Hill He Calls Home, by John B. Lee – #1
Calling The Wild, by Roger Hilles – #2
Riding On A Magpie Riff, by Richard Stevenson – #3
When The Earth Was Flat, Raymond Fraser – #4
Left Hand Horses, John B. Lee – #5
The Gargoyle's Left Ear, by Susan McMaster – #6

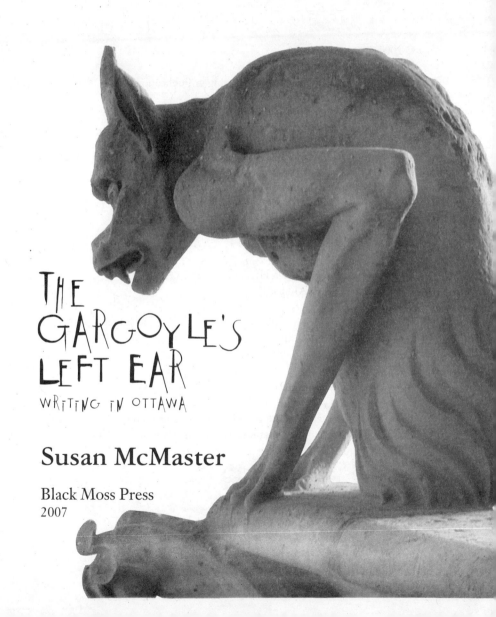

THE GARGOYLE'S LEFT EAR

WRITING IN OTTAWA

Susan McMaster

Black Moss Press
2007

© 2007 Susan McMaster

Library and Archives Canada Cataloguing in Publication

McMaster, Susan
   The gargoyle's left ear: writing in Ottawa / Susan McMaster.

Includes index.
ISBN 978-0-88753-443-0

   I. Title.

PS8573.M33G37 2007   C818'.54   C2007-904128-0

Author photo, at La Roche d'Hys, 2007: Marty Gervais
Design: Karen Veryle Monck

Black Moss Press is published at 2450 Byng Road, Windsor, Ontario, Canada
N8W 3E8. Black Moss books are distributed in Canada and the U.S. by
LitDistco. All orders should be directed there.

Black Moss can be contacted on its website at www.blackmosspress.com.

Black Moss acknowledges the generous support for its publishing program
from The Canada Council for the Arts and The Ontario Arts Council.

Le Conseil des Arts | The Canada Council
du Canada | for the Arts

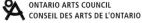

ONTARIO ARTS COUNCIL
CONSEIL DES ARTS DE L'ONTARIO

Acknowledgments

My warm thanks, in this first prose venture, to Marty Gervais, embodiment of Black Moss, who asked me to do the book, convinced me I could, and supported me all the way; to Renate Mohr, whose creative reading was crucial; to my daughter Morel, whose insights on early drafts informed the rest; to writers Betsy Struthers, Ronnie R. Brown, and Mary Lee Bragg, who gave me generous "been there" guidance; to my friend Gwen Frankton, who swore she couldn't put it down; to my parents, Gordon and Betty, who didn't ask me to change a thing; to poet and editor John B. Lee, whose intelligent restructuring made all the difference; to my daughter Aven, who always asked; and to my husband, Ian, who read, contributed, and, above all, lived with it and me through every blessed and depressed moment. My gratitude goes out as always to family and friends, named or not – all are appreciated. Warm thanks as well to Howard Aster, who welcomed me with food, wine, and a wonderful view at La Roche d'Hys in France in the last deadline week.

Beyond the book, I would like to offer my continuing gratitude to those collaborators who have joined me throughout the years, and to the readers, audiences, media, writers' groups, and funding organizations that have supported my projects.

The Gargoyle's Left Ear is for you.

Contents

Walking home one night...

Continuing Lines

Walking home one night along Colonel By, just past the bridge where there used to be a colony of blankets and dogs and low voices and pinched cigarettes, walking in the middle of the grass rather than on the paved path because it's one of those nights, those Ottawa nights when the air is full of scent and soft as a feather pillow on your skin, and the sky is almost black but not quite because it's just an hour after the late, late July sunset, so a bit of indigo glass hangs where the sky should be…

Walking through the grass, coming from a reading or a gathering or a book event, some such mix of people and words of the kind I so enjoy, something accomplished, something to come, and all so fine…

I think: this is my town. This is my place. I know that gather of crab apple trees, blossoms still drifting a few pale petals down among the remnants of white narcissus, the long-gone crocuses (I'd followed them too). I know that bench, where first love and I leaned into the small hours breathing lifetime promises. Over there, that's where I turn my bicycle every morning and every evening to follow the curving route from home to work, door to door, the water and park route that is one of the many that braid the city with their clear, open paths and garden-banked roads, that make driving even in rush hour a bird-full thing, or a matter of mist, or snow heaps, or sun skip-stepping over slanted waves.

I know this town. Behind me the Peace Tower dozes over all, its gargoyles awake and frowning on guard. Those stairs mark the way to the bar on Laurier Avenue where poets gather every week or two for a half of beer and a turn to read. Just up that block is the corner of Main where the best vegetarian restaurant in town is found, beyond that is the bridge to the Pretoria Loblaws and its flanking flower stalls, beer and wine stores, and handy bank machine. There's the checkerboard of turns through the stop-signed Glebe past the lagoon where I skate every winter, the school that was my kindergarten, the store no longer there where I spent my twenty-five cents on sour candies and red licorice. Every step I take deepens another one of mine from two or five or forty years ago, strengthens this feeling of here-ness, of mine, of these are the people I know, these are the smells in my poetry, the sidewalks that scraped my bare feet as a child...

Walking home tonight, jubilation fills me like summer ice cream.

First Lines

Gargoyle: a carved human or animal face or figure
projecting from the edge of a roof of (especially a Gothic) building,
usually as a spout to carry water clear of a wall.

– Canadian Oxford Dictionary

Branching Out

Nothing is simple, some things are good.

A line that brings with it a vivid memory of writing by candlelight at a picnic table in a campground in the Rocky Mountains in 1971. Strange to start a book about Ottawa so far away. And yet, this evening was the beginning of many things: collaboration, writing projects, social activism, above all, my life of writing poetry. It was the first time I had ever gone away, entirely on my own, to write. The young men at the next campsite were whooping it up along with the truck radio, the ping-pong-ball-sized Rocky Mountain mosquitoes were finally settling down after "mosquito moment," and I looked up in the long Alberta evening at the peaks still capped in late sunlight, and tried to capture how I felt.

This is our first time away from Ottawa, for Ian and me both. Married in 1969, we came to Edmonton in 1971 so Ian could do his Master of Computing Science at the University of Alberta. Now he's busy ten, fourteen, eighteen hours a day with his studies. I use my new Elementary Teacher's Certificate to teach a two-tenths load: in Alberta, just like Ontario, there are too few children and too many teachers. The rest of the day I'm on my own. The first winter, we lived in a little, white, freezing bungalow at the edge of campus, and I read every Harlequin Romance that came in to the drugstore next door, sometimes two a day; since coming here, I've gulped down about 250. Marriage is different than I thought it would be. Other than Harlequins, there's *Good Housekeeping*, *Redbook*, *Cosmopolitan*. *Chatelaine* is still the only Canadian choice.

"*Ms. Magazine* is good, but it's American. There's nothing like it here." Feminism is spreading even to Canada, even to the west, but I feel left out.

This fall, in 1972, Ian and I moved to a co-op house on 77th Avenue, and are now walking home along the broad expanse of 118 Street. Roads are so wide in the west. The hardy crab apple and plum trees that line the pavement survived a winter that stayed below minus thirty degrees during the days for a whole month, and minus fifty and colder at night. The trees are in full, fragrant bloom.

"What we need," I continue grouchily, "is a new magazine, something that talks about Edmonton, about Ottawa, about the people and places we know. I want something to read!"

I've just finished *Surfacing*, Margaret Atwood's novel about a woman in the northern woods. It hit me like a load of pulpwood falling off a logging truck. A Canadian writer. A Canadian woman writer, just ten years older than I am, writing with such authority, clarity, richness – poetry turned to prose. I've pasted a magazine photo of her inside the cover of my writing binder.

"So start one."

"One what?" My thoughts have been wandering to the brightest spot in my week: the creative writing class with poet Doug Barbour and novelist W.O. Mitchell. *The Gateway*, the University of Alberta student paper, is about to publish several of my poems.

"A magazine. Start a feminist women's magazine, like you're talking about."

It takes only six more blocks and a dozen more showers of crab apple petals before I've grabbed onto the idea as my own, and we're in full planning mode.

"We could have stories and poetry, too, not just articles. The old magazines always did. And what about artwork, or photos?"

"Do you know a photographer?" he asks.

A friend has a silkscreen press, and one colour of ink. He helps us make two dozen day-glo pink announcements and I post them on telephone poles around campus.

A week later, some thirty women and a few men crowd into the co-op living room. The first group decision, that the magazine will be run only by women, means the men and a few women don't return the next week. The second is choosing a name; in the end, that takes weeks and weeks. In this first meeting, though, the main problem in the loud babble of excitement is writing all the ideas down.

"There's a woman at the university, Aritha van Herk …"

"My friend Jane Rule might send something…"

"Why don't we ask Margaret Atwood, you never know…"

"Or Dorothy Livesay…"

"What about native issues…"

"Elizabeth Brewster's always helpful…"

"Margaret Laurence will be here next month…"

Seventeen of us stick it out through the next three months. We learn everything from scratch. We ask, and Margaret Atwood does send us two unpublished poems for the preview issue, and we accept poems from Polly Steele (who's in my writing class) and C.M. Buckaway. I don't submit any of my own poetry: I don't want a vanity publication. We ask Dorothy Livesay, and she contributes a short story; Sonja Chandra sends another. Jan Andrews submits a children's tale illustrated by Linda Donnelly. We receive a letter of support from Margaret Laurence, and prominent journalist June

Sheppard interviews her for the issue. Book reviews come in from poet Susan Musgrave and Maureen Scobie, as well as articles on "Indian Rights for Indian Women" by Jenny Margetts, on latch-key kids by Judith Kirstein, on Galician centenarian Miriam Elston by journalist Dorothy Dahlgren, and on champion trap-shooter Sue Nattrass by me. There are photo features on the art of Eva Diener by Jetske Sybesma Ironside and on that of Hakon Jossiassen by staff member Alice Baumann-Rondez (who also does the cover photo); artwork by Eileen Taylor, illustrations by Ironside, by staff member Iona MacAllister, and by Ann Powell; an opinion column by staff member Roberta Kalechofsky; a "here and there" announcement column by us all; and a list of publications and women's centres across Canada from a project I did with the Alberta government my first summer. I write an editorial explaining the name we've finally chosen, *Branching Out*: it's meant to represent a winter tree about to burst into leaf. Luckily, Letraset offers an image we can use as a logo (although I've since wondered if the existence of the logo determined the name). Letters of support arrive from Isabel Munroe, the Dean of Women at the university, from Anne Lambert of the Alberta Options for Women Council, and from Dona Harvey at the *Edmonton Journal*. We have nine ads: from bookstores; from food and clothing stores, including a back cover from Horne and Pitfield Foods; and from CBC radio's "As It Happens," a whole third of a page.

This level of contribution and support is astounding for a preview issue of a non-commercial publication. Almost every budding feminist and prominent professional woman in town hears about it, and wants to help. As we go to press, I realize that, in fact, *Branching Out* is the first national feminist magazine in Canada. (Even *Room of One's Own*, that doyenne of Canadian literary feminism, didn't appear for several more years.)

Other staff listed in the preview issue of December 1973 are Sharon Batt, Beverley Brown, Gwen Brown, Mary Alyce Heaton, Terri Jackson, Lynn Jacobs, Naomi Loeb, Helen Rosta, Donaleen Saul, and Meg Shatilla. The issue sells for a dollar, and is stocked in Edmonton by the campus bookstore and a few others. I bring it back to Ottawa at Christmas and take it to Prospero Books and Shirley Leishman's, which agree to stock it for a fellow Ottawan.

Peter Gzowski of CBC "Morningside" fame gives me eleven minutes on national radio not long after the preview issue comes out because I phone to complain they're featuring a new Canadian girly magazine, so why not us? Our subscriptions triple overnight. I get lambasted by one of the contributors for stealing all the glory and not mentioning anyone else in the interview. Eleven minutes, with my knees shaking, and I didn't list all seventeen of us. My first acid taste of the hidden difficulties of a "consensual" and "egalitarian" project.

There are other setbacks. A major grocery chain arranges to stock the magazine on its shelves – except that the first issue contains the word *fuck* so they cancel. This gives me a chance to write an energetic editorial for the next issue.

Ian and I return to Ottawa when he finishes his degree in 1975, and Sharon Batt takes over as editor. At loose ends, I decide to learn how to do all the things I've been doing for three years, so sign up for a master's degree in journalism at Carleton. Encouraged by professor Joe Scanlan, I intend to document *Branching Out* for my thesis, but my eventual advisor thinks I'm "too close" to the topic, and neither thesis nor degree are ever finished.

The same year I give up on mastering anything, 1980, *Branching Out* publishes its last issue. It is, in the end, impossible to keep such a venture going on the backs of volunteers – even though there are 4500 subscribers across the country when it folds. The story of the magazine is too long to tell in full here, but I hope someone will write it up one day. Women still approach me from time to time to say that their first published poem or story or artwork appeared in *Branching Out*.

I look up from the past, and across the lake. Twenty-five years later, I sit again by myself on a writing retreat, this time in the "wooden tent" of our cottage on Lac Vert in Quebec, two hours west and north of Ottawa. The sun, just edging down over the hill opposite, sends a spill of cherry-koolaid across my table. Two loons chat in short little whoops. Time to hunker down with a book before the fire. At least that overdose of Harlequins in Edmonton burned romance novels out of my system. That and *Branching Out*. I find it interesting that Atwood published *Lady Oracle*, a spoof about a gothic romance writer's real love life, in 1976, at the heyday of our magazine.

As for myself, how would I sum it all up, thirty years later? *Nothing is simple*, I write. *Some things are good.*

First Draft

The main branch of the Ottawa Public Library is where I did the first performance poetry presentation of my life — in fact, my first reading.

My brother Andrew lives over a store that sells mirrors, and my white face slips along beside me as I head for his door. It's 12 November 1981. Last year he came back from studies in composition and cello in Germany, and we've been meeting weekly since. Ostensibly it was so my three-year-old daughter, Aven, could have a piano lesson, though what she really likes is the brie cheese and smoked oysters Andrew serves me afterwards. And I come for the talk: talk about his music and my poetry and the difficulty and complications of simply doing them. My problem is too much other life, plus lack of confidence. Andrew's problem is too little money, so that he works at a variety of jobs that constantly distract him from writing music. And we both fight major anxiety about our work.

Together, we are learning to cope with this. One trick is scratching our To-Do lists and replacing them with Done lists. Another is getting together with others. After I have my second daughter, Morel, in February 1980, the afternoon meetings become too difficult, so we've begun to meet instead at the R&R restaurant at the corner of Bank and Holmwood. Every Monday evening, we drink beer and coffee, beer and coffee, alternately, and invite anyone we know who's involved in the arts to join us. We have no plans, no intentions. The only rule is, everyone has to talk for a few minutes about their current project. We've adopted the name First Draft for our loose group as a mild joke on the draft beer and the draft poems and artworks and ideas that crossed the table.

Another trick is blending our media. Not long ago, we managed a weekend away at the cottage on Lac Vert. I almost set my hair on fire, we got lost in the woods for two hours – and we began to play with one of my poems in a musical way. We've decided to face down our nervousness by staging a First Draft First Annual Group Show, of my poetry and Andrew's music along with art by Claude Dupuis and Gwen Frankton. At this weekend, we were considering what music might match what poems, when Andrew came up with the brilliant idea of notating the poems as spoken "songs." He sketched out a setting for my very short poem "shadowless / on black spruce / shrike swoops" using three voices in the form of a round, as well as notations for timbre (from whisper to half-voice to normal to focussed voice), loudness, and pitch (high or low within the performer's normal spoken range). We've decided to call the form wordmusic, and are very excited about it. Andrew has set several more poems of mine for spoken voice for the performance, so that's a "done."

Many friends have come through to help. On stage we'll have me, plus Ruth Pinco (soprano), Elizabeth Griffiths (French horn), Andrew (violoncello), and Glen Carruthers (voice, although he's actually a pianist). We've all bought outfits from Sarah Clothes, the import and designer shop unique to Ottawa, gauzy pleated skirts and tops and sashes and shirts in rich colours; Andrée Pouliot has given us a discount. The musicians will join us as voices in the wordmusic pieces. I'll read some poems solo, Andrew and friends will present some of his musical compositions.

We've found a space in the auditorium at the main Ottawa Public Library at Metcalfe and Laurier. Gwen and Claude are right now hanging her fabric art and his paintings outside the auditorium. My sister-in-law Marie McMaster, a graphic artist, has designed the poster and program. Others listed there include volunteers David Peebles, Michael Phelan, Stephanie Martin, Joann Charpentier, Shannon Lee Mannion, and Stephen Gower; and patrons and friends Mary McClure, Betty McClure, Gilles Frappier, Maurice Gagnon, Alrick Huebener, Harold Lubert, Martha McClure, Gordon McClure, Arthur McGregor, Nancy and Eric McMaster, Nick and Lise Orfanos, Marie Piché, Susan Taylor, the Folklore Centre, M.F. McHugh School, Place Muzik, Prospero Books, Sarah Clothes, and Merle Norman Cosmetics.

For Andrew and me, the poster was the hardest. Who are we to stand beside Dickinson and Bach? By keeping the possibility of running away to Mexico firmly in mind, we have been able to do it: there it is in bold black and white, Susan McMaster – poet, Andrew McClure – composer. Come and see what we do.

Today we are meeting one last time, just like the old days, in the quiet of the apartment, to reassure each other and ourselves before the big night – tonight. Everyone is helping us, and everyone we know will be there. All our eggs in one basket.

I snatch up the last piece of brie before Aven can get it, and eat it all.

The hall was packed, the show a success. Our eggs survived uncracked, and over the next decade we painted them in a rainbow of colours.

Probably thirty people passed through First Draft between 1980 and 1990 or so. Artists, dancers, writers, composers, theatre people. I met poet Colin Morton at a Tree reading – the series was being held in the Quaker Meeting House on Fourth Avenue at the time – and he became our third central performing member, writing, publishing, and presenting wordmusic and intermedia shows with us throughout the eighties. Claude continued to come by, and Gwen when she was in town, sculptor John Tappin came a few times, and poet Nan Cormier, composer David Parsons, Alrick and Roberta Huebener, and Peter Thomas became regulars, among many others.

We did a second annual show at Theatre 2000 and performed in dozens of galleries, cafés, music venues, schools, and libraries in Ottawa, Toronto, Peterborough, and around – anywhere someone knew someone. Colin and Andrew and I toured Canada with the help of Gwen Hoover and the Canada Council (which cobbled together a category for intermedia under her guidance). We played in places like the Banff Centre, and came back to record a full-length professional audiotape of wordmusic and music with Paula Quick and Open Score. Other groups like Girigonza and Earlick performed and recorded our work, including the "Science Songs" Andrew later wrote around my "Dark Galaxies" poem series. We were broadcast on local radio (Sharon Burke at Chez also made a tape for us) and tv (and Carleton made a video) and on national radio shows like CBC's Morningside with Peter Gzowski again, bless him, and Two New Hours.

When Ian and I were in Europe for his sabbatical in 1984, Colin and his publishing house, Ouroboros, published *The Scream: First Draft, the third annual group show*, an interactive anthology of poetry, music scores, flip art, wordmusic, bios, and photography which bpNichol thought was "fabulous."

Wordmusic

Which brings me to bpNichol and the Four Horsemen and the Great Canadian Writers' Weekend at Collingwood in 1982.

I've just seen the Horsemen perform, and am still quivering from the excitement and energy of their presentation. I've driven in from Ottawa this morning with Ronnie R. Brown and Sheila McCarthy: we were matched up for the trip by the organizers. We all have poems published – in the conference anthology for one thing – but no book yet.

bp, on the other hand, is a star. He won a Governor-General's award in his twenties, and has by now, in his thirties, so many books and recordings and projects that they're impossible to track (jw curry will later spend much of his life trying to do this; as of 2007, the list is still not complete). bpNichol is *it* in sound poetry in Canada.

And very popular. He's leaning on the small bar of the hotel after the show, drinking a beer, surrounded by well wishers and raising a hand or exchanging greetings with poets I know only by reputation, like Margaret Atwood and Graeme Gibson. I have no place in that group, but I can't stay away: the power of the performance, the clearly visible warmth and kindness of the man, the fact above all that he is doing a version of what Andrew and I are working on in First Draft in our wordmusic – working with many voices together as sound as well as meaning – draw me towards him.

The crowd is thinning. I edge closer, introduce myself. I don't know quite how it happens, but we're talking not about sound poetry, but about travel and the weekend. He's staying only till tomorrow morning, to hear the non-star reading (this is typical, I discover: his interest in new voices, the diffident beginners), and is aching to get away and back to his wife, Ellie, and their just born infant daughter, Sarah. The same first name as my daughter Aven's. How old is she now, how was the birth? This is what bp really wants to talk about tonight: his enthusiasm, joy, tumble out in an rush of visible love for Ellie and Sarah, his worry and care, his urgent wish to be with them, hold his baby...

Yes. I know. We're both turning our shoulders now to others who come along wanting to talk about, of all things, poetry.

Only after he sags a little, talks of bed, of phoning home, do I remember to tell him about our wordmusic. Briefly. I can see how tired he is. Tell him that I've brought three trio pieces to perform, and ask him – how do I get the courage, but then he's a father now, after all – if he'll join me and Ronnie to perform the poems at the open mic.

Ah, he's heard such requests before.

"Bring me the score at breakfast, and I'll see."

Pass this way again, North/South, Dark Galaxies

*All my stories about bpNichol, except the last, have a happy ending. He did join us, reading Andrew's new notation instantly. Not long after, he sent me his chapbook **still**, and I wrote back. In a few months, I visited him – and Ellie and Sarah – with a complete manuscript of my poems, accompanied by Andrew's wordmusic scores: **Pass this way again**. Hoping for comment, maybe a bit of encouragement among the criticism.*

"I'll do it," he says, turning the pages.

"You'll what?"

"I'll publish the book. With Underwhich. Send me the camera ready copy and we'll go to press."

It is possibly the happiest day of my life. Floating, leaping, giggling, practically cartwheeling across the street to the bus station after he drives me to the corner, I can't believe it. I have a book coming out, of my own poetry, with a real publisher, edited by bpNichol.

This is the beginning of the most fruitful and precious literary friendship of my life.

Claude Dupuis designs *Pass this way again* and pulls it together, with a dozen of his own graphite drawings and Andrew's handwritten musical scores, and it's launched in 1983 by our friends the Martins in their party room. I get very drunk, out of pure exhilaration and relief. Oh dear. Underwhich still has *Pass* on its catalogue; sometimes inquiries come in from people looking for books on reincarnation.

They also have the *Wordmusic* recording we go on to do, and the second score book, *North/South*, which bp publishes in 1986. He comes to Ottawa to help us launch it, at a gallery on the market.

Pretty well no-one turns up, which I find humiliating but beep takes in stride, teaching me a thing or two. Colin Morton has joined us by then and the book features his poetry and wordmusic as well as mine and Andrew's. Susan Feindel's art is on the cover, and Roberta Huebener does all the calligraphy and design this time. It takes her nine months. Music writing programs don't exist in the eighties.

bp, like Colin and Alrick and Peter and Claude, is a friend simply, so that at one point I think, my life is full of men and I'm not sleeping with any of them. A change from the wild girl who was. In that way, First Draft is also a feminist, a humanist, adventure, in which I and the other women involved are there not as ornaments or organizers and the men are there not as Cool Lukes or *artistes*. We are all collaborators on equal terms – people, in fact.

The Collingwood weekend also led to me editing Ronnie's book *Re Creations* for Balmuir, an Ottawa press run by Alex Inglis, who eventually married Andrew. I also edited Ottawa poet Stephen Brockwell's first book, *The Wire in Fences*, and *Dangerous Graces*, a poetry script I wrote for a performance at the Great Canadian Theatre Company, for that press. Claude did the covers for all three books; Andrew wrote and played the music for the stage show; Ronnie came up with the title for both show and book and contributed poems to each.

After Andrew moved to Toronto with Alex in the late eighties, it just wasn't the same. Director-dramaturge Jen Boyes and I had worked with Andrew on the GCTC show, and on the Page to Stage workshopping of my play *Dark Galaxies* at the National Arts Centre Atelier. We tried to mount a full production of it, but just couldn't hold the creative process together across two cities. Proximity matters.

First Draft dissolved for good around 1991. The mirror store is still there, on Bank Street north of the Queensway, though the R&R has been replaced by a Pizza Pizza. After it closed, we never again found the perfect spot to meet and talk, a place without the loud music in the background, a place to drink endless cups of whatever without emptying our pockets. That restaurant was important to everything that happened. The biggest show we ever did with First Draft involved some dozen performers, plus a whole back-up crew. We held the post-show party at the R&R, and Nick and Lise contributed a round of beer for everyone – about sixty people. It was a fine place, and I've never found a satisfactory replacement. If you know of one, please tell me. I'm thinking of starting another group...

27

Dark Galaxies

Having given up on a master of journalism, I receive, instead, a mystery of poetry from bpNichol.

Even while First Draft is filling every crack, I'm still trying to pull together my first solo poetry book. No-one is interested. I start a scrapbook of rejections – at least it gives me the kindergarten consolation of cut-and-paste. Some of the letters say nice things; others, I edit.

And now, I've met bp. Not quite realizing what an imposition it might be, I phone him up one day and ask if I can visit and show him a few poems. It's harder to refuse someone on the phone than on email, and soon I'm travelling to Toronto every few months with a new batch.

He meets me every time with warmth and full attention, as does his wife, Ellie, perhaps the kindest person in the world. Though she of course is entirely innocent of involvement, in a sideways way I think of Sarah as my muse, since it was through her that bp and I became friends (he said once, don't call me a mentor, I don't like that, we're friends), and I bring her a small animal toy. Either Sarah, or bp, likes these or pretends to, I never do find out which.

Thus begins a painstaking process of working through every poem I can dig up, line by line. I learn that the true editor brings out the author's voice, not his own. That the appropriate range of comment is from "doesn't work" to "fabulous" (bp doesn't offer too many of the latter until I begin to understand the former). I learn to leap off the end of a poem instead of tying it neatly up. "Today I turned everything around" starts as a whine in the voice of a repressed little complainer flipping a few rugs, and ends, under his tutelage, as the roar of a giantess crushing the house in her fist and waving it over her faithless lover's head. That poem gains sinew and loses restrictive details, so that I'll go on to read it at union rallies, peace marches, feminist events, even a Nova Scotia jam as a poem about housework. Universality, taught to me in specifics.

But there's more to a book than its contents. Now I have a number of poems, but no shape to the manuscript, and no publisher. Colin steps in. Along with his wife, Mary Lee Bragg, he's decided to start a poetry press, Ouroboros. Colin himself is a fine poet, and he has an additional, rare, quality: the analytical eye that can make sense of porridge. His offer to publish a book of mine sends me again leaping and cavorting through the streets like a nanny goat with a pepper up her bum – but it's just the start. At this point, *Dark Galaxies* is a cobble of poems from those classes with W.O. Mitchell and Doug Barbour at the University of Alberta in 1972, from workshops with Miriam Waddington at Canadore College (her advice to me: Cut, cut, cut!) and Chris Levenson at Carleton in the mid seventies, through my first litmag publication by Stephen Gill in *Writers' Lifeline* in 1981, to the new science series (which will eventually provide the book's title). They may have been already run through bp's wringer, but Colin turns a severe and shaping eye on the revised poems and chooses only the best. He also edits them further, adding subtle refinements.

And the book is beautiful, a family affair. Roberta designs the cover. Ian takes the photo of me, intent in my writing tent at Lac Vert. Colin asks bp for back-cover copy, and he writes a few words. They still give me hope.

Dark Galaxies comes out with Ouroboros in 1986, and receives a few decent reviews, some sales, some notice. A good beginning.

And then what? How to match that, go farther? Surely it won't take another ten years.

30

Life Lines

Among England's richest array of gargoyles – on the
fourteenth-century parish church at Heckington, Lincolnshire –
is an elegantly dressed woman holding an open book.
Traditionally, women were not supposed to take knowledge
into their own hands.

– Michael Camille, *Images on the Edge*
(London: Reaktion, 1992), p. 80

Central Canada Exhibition

When I was a child, we lived in a series of row houses in the Glebe, now mostly replaced by apartment buildings which are themselves beginning to sag at the knees. None had backyards, but we were across the street from the park that ran along the Rideau Canal and just a few blocks from the Exhibition Grounds.

"Parking for a dollar, parking for a dollar."

I wave my cardboard box-flap with its scribbled offer at the cars cruising slowly towards me. The first one pulls over. Four kids hang on the back seat and bounce up and down behind their mother and their father, who skids his wheels as he steers over the bump of the sidewalk and onto our front lawn.

Three quarters, two dimes, and a nickel. This is our fifth car since morning, and now we have enough money to go the Ex. I wake Dad from his nap, and we head off, me holding my younger brother Peter by the hand, Dad lagging behind trying to light his pipe.

We follow the link fence around the exhibition grounds, past the back of the show tents and trailers to the entrance booth at Bank Street. Boys and girls like me walk horses and cows and sheep in the narrow space behind the fence, or brush them with flat brushes like the ones we use on shoes. The smell of popcorn and hotdogs and cotton candy and cigarettes blows through the wire mesh.

Ten cents for a child, twenty-five for my dad. We get a dollar each to spend. The barkers on the midway shout so loudly it's hard to tell what they're saying. Some tents we can't enter, of course, like the ones with women outside in high heels and shiny bathing suits. Others, like the House of Mirrors, might be fun but would use up half my money. A man in a checkered shirt and jeans swings around holding a stuffed white bear, and almost hits me; he hands it to a woman with bright yellow hair, who kisses the bear, leaving a red mark.

Peter pulls us to a stop in front of the Tilt-a-Whirl, which starts to spin and then rises on its edge into the air till the riders are pressed flat against the sky. "I want to go on that one," he says.

"Let's go see the cows and pigs first." I can tell Dad's stalling.

In the Cattle Castle, which looks like a Zeller's birthday cake on the outside, all coloured twirls and squiggles, but smells like a farm inside, Dad lets us run down the aisles ahead of him.

"Hey look, at this one –" The black bull snorts, spraying Peter with little drops, and he scoots back to my side.

"What about these baby pigs?" We pull ouselves up on the edge of the wooden stall. Piglets like little pink ponies, skinny and graceful, skitter around the clean straw on polished hooves.

The long flat Food Exhibition building is a break from the sun now blazing noon at us, and a place for free samples. Cheese, crackers, and – bingo! – chocolates. We buy hotdogs from one stand, and a cardboard cup of lemonade, made in front of us out of real lemons, from another.

I decide on the pony ride, two slow clomps around a circle. I pat the pony and talk to it, but its eyes are covered with leather blinkers. It doesn't flick an ear.

Peter chooses the junior roller coaster, and shouts when it goes over the big bump.

We still have enough money to buy candy floss. For me, this is the best part of the Exhibition. I love watching the man swirl the paper cone around the tub, twisting it up into a cloud. Peter launches into his nose first. Dad eats puffs of floss around puffs of smoke; pink threads stick in his beard. I can never decide whether to eat the sugary strands as they are, filled with air, or whether to squash them up into a chewy pink glob first.

And then Peter's back at the Tilt-a-Whirl.

"Dad, what if he gets sick?"

But my father's already talking to the ticket-seller. The motor starts to hum and then roar, the music gets louder, and the platform rises, tilts on its side. I can see Peter holding on tight, his eyes pressed shut.

When he staggers down the ramp, he's white. "That was fun," he says.

I stare at him. "If Peter can go on the Tilt-a-Whirl, I can go on the Ferris wheel."

The operator is doubtful. In the end, he will only agree if Dad comes too. The seat is slippery metal mesh that rocks and swings as we get in. The operator pulls a bar down in front of us, but it's not even locked into place. Peter is staring up at us – we're already above his head. Dad's pipe has gone out.

Dum-de-dum-de-boom-boom... A sudden roar of music, and we start to rise.

"I don't think I want to do this, Dad!"

"You can't get off now."

I shut my eyes.

Suddenly we jerk to a stop. I squeeze one eyelid apart. We're at the very top and our seat is swinging back and forth! My stomach drops out of me like a gush of ice water.

"Daddy!" He's gripping the bar with both hands and won't even look at me. The motor starts to hum again...

By the time we finish the long drop I'm screaming so hard I can barely breathe. The operator has to let us off. He yanks up the bar and I stumble out. He pulls my father on the arm to make him move.

"And take your pipe with you!" The man kicks the stem and bowl, which have fallen in two pieces to the ground.

As we head out the main gates, Peter pulls away from Dad's hand and drops back beside me.

"I don't feel so good," I say.

"Tilt-a-Girl," my brother whispers, as I bend over and start to throw up.

Glebites can no longer park cars on their lawns, but the Exhibition still arrives each year, along with other loud events, from football games like my first date with Ian, to rock concerts that boom across the Canal to shake the windows of the "blue room" where I write. Ian and I recently framed the poster we pulled from the Civic Centre wall as Pierre Trudeau began his rise at Canada's first pop-star political convention in 1968.

And still, from time to time, we go to the Ex, to see the cows and quilts, to graze on the free samples in the food building, to push through the grease and glitter of the midway. I never go on a ride. One day I'll take my grandchildren along, for pony rides and merry-go-rounds, for hot dogs and lemonade, for piglets and bulls.

Mainly, though, for the candy floss.

Rideau Canal

The year I turned eight, the park around the Lily Pond, just alongside the Rideau Canal at the foot of Third Avenue, became my favourite place to loll.

It's a dozing hazy spring day, too warm to stay indoors. I haven't been to school now for almost two months. The doctor says we have to stay home, my brother and I, at least until school is over. All I do in class anyway is read under the desk, and now I don't need to hide my book. We have mononucleosis – which I've learned how to spell. The kids at school call it "kissing sickness," though the only people I kiss are my family, and none of them is ill, except my mom, who says she doesn't have time for it.

The cure for mono is rest. At first all I want to do is sleep. By the time I feel better, it's April and edging towards full spring. We're steps from the Driveway, so on a day like this we shuffle over to the park and spread our blanket on the grassy bank by the Lily Pond. We've packed a banana and two apples and some raisins and cheese. Mom's just left, saying we're old enough to take care of ourselves for an hour. Right now I'm watching two mothers with babies. They're sitting on a bench facing the Lily Pond and rocking the carriages with their feet: I can hear the soft squeaks; one baby has started to make a sound like my kitten. A couple of toddlers at the edge of the pond have a glass jar, which they're dipping into the water. I've done that too – collected the tadpoles that swim in the mud among the waterlily stems, watched them grow little black legs and arms for a few days, then tipped them back into the water.

An old man is reading a newspaper on a bench facing the Canal. It's blue and smooth from here, but I know if I go closer there's a smell like our kitchen sink. Sometimes I have a nightmare about falling in. I poke my brother as the old man's paper slips lower and lower, till he wakes up with a jerk. If I felt better today, I'd climb that big willow behind him, climb up on the roots that bulge from the ground, and scramble along one of the two low slanted trunks and to the branch above his head. I'd sit there, brushed by new willow leaves on tiny yellow twigs with the small flute of a sparrow piping above me, and read my book, and no-one would see me.

There are other willows up and down the canal, but this is my favourite. In an hour, school will be out. Boys will drop their bikes on the grass around the trunk, and girlfriends holding hands will sit and giggle on the humps of roots. They all go to First Avenue Public School, the sturdy brick building at the corner of O'Connor, and sometimes a friend from class will come over with a map I'm supposed to colour in, or a sheet of arithmetic for my brother. Our parents are teachers, and even ill, it seems to them, we should do a little something.

A worker with a pullcart and spike passes us, stabbing and bagging cigarette packages and chocolate bar wrappings. My brother is drawing a crocus – there are three purple ones and a yellow bud growing near us, plus a lot of green spikes without flowers yet. He draws a lot. I have a page of spelling to learn, and some comprehension problems.

It gives me a vague, satisfied feeling of accomplishing something to do these things, and in such a lazy, dreaming way that it seems no effort.

But what intrigues me most, right at this moment, is the exact look and feel of a paper-thin, over-wintered maple leaf in the grass by my hand, washed of colour but with a fine skiff of dusty, translucent tissue between tiny veins splayed from a central rib. Today, in the slow long sunny afternoon, with my brother quiet and friendly beside me, I drift, and lie.

I still travel along the Canal to work and back each day, walk along it in times of happiness and trouble. Even the dead fish smell of spring is welcome, an invitation to climb over the iron railings to track crayfish and snails on the exposed mud and poke through debris like broken wooden crates and single rubber boots before the waterway is filled for summer. I was walking home along the Canal one evening, in my twenties, exalted after an exuberant reading by Anne Szumigalski, a Governor-General's-award-winning poet from Saskatchewan. The lines I wrote that night under a street light by the water end:

> crayfish
> bared in the spring mud
> their claws
> their fishy smell.

I left out the boots.

Bank Street

The Canal marked the east boundary of the Glebe I knew, and Bank Street marked the west, with O'Connor bisecting the middle. We moved up and down within the six-block square between First and Fourth Avenues seven times in thirteen years, as the family grew and we needed more room. Always, we were close to Bank Street.

By 1960, at nine and a half, I'm the oldest of six, and I often do some of the shopping. I head up Second Avenue towards Bank, paper dollar scrunched in the mitten strung up my sleeve to its mate on the other arm, snowpants pulled over galoshes, coat buttoned to the neck, scarf wound around my nose. I'm off to buy three pounds of hamburger for a dollar, a staple of our large family – for meatloaf, or hash, or spaghetti – my favourite. Mom likes making spaghetti best because you don't have to peel it.

The February afternoon is dark and the old houses set back behind their verandahs are dim. Elm trees clump black against a nickel sky. A streetcar hums and rattles up Bank, whines to a stop. One awful day, on this same errand, I lost a ten-dollar bill – enough to feed our family for a week. Keeping my fist closed on the dollar bill, I run around the corner to beat the cold, skid to the lit windows between Second and Third, push open the heavy glass door. The Glebe Meat Market. There's a soft, bright kind of smell in here, like the grass after it rains. Maybe it comes from the open freezer at the side, or the glistening piles of meat behind the glass counter. The man cutting slices of baloney with a whirring machine glances up as I enter, and frowns.

"Good evening," I say politely, like the grown-up women do. "May I have three pounds of hamburger, please?"

Suddenly, he grins. "Certainly, Madam."

He waves me towards a black-haired boy behind the counter. The boy looks at me sideways as he scoops red curls from a mound into shiny brown paper, folds over the corners, ties the package with string. I reach up over the counter with my squashed dollar bill, and he stretches to meet me. Our fingers touch as we exchange handfuls.

And I'm out the door. A scatter of snow is beginning to skip through the streetlights, which turn on one by one, making columns of frosty yellow against the black sky. I'm running now, because the wind is behind me, because I'm hungry and alive, because the street looks strange and shadowy between the circles of light. All the doors along the way are closed, no-one is out, except one old lady carrying a paper bag and a package like mine. She's climbing the steps to her verandah, and the cat at her feet is meowing. Maybe they're having spaghetti, too.

The Glebe Meat Market is now at the corner of Regent and Bank. These days they sell duck eggs and caribou, grain-fed chicken and loin pork roast, but I've come in this Saturday for Yuppie hamburger – lean ground round – which costs a lot more than thirty-three cents a pound. The place is full of balloons and banners and television cameras: it seems the Market is celebrating its fiftieth birthday. I stay out of the lights, but can't resist telling one of the cheerful men packaging my meat that I've been buying here off and on since 1956, when I was six years old. He's a handsome black-haired man, showing a few streaks of grey. Several other staff have similar good looks.

"Since 1956?," he says, with a broad smile, stepping out from behind the counter to bring my meat to the cash. "Did you hear that, this lady has been coming here since 1956!"

He open his arms wide, presents me like a prize fillet of steak to the crowd of customers and staff and tv crew. I take a small bow.

"Happy Birthday! I hope you and your store are here for another fifty years."

"Madame, with customers like you, we will be!"

The lady at the cash – his wife, his daughter? – shakes her head and laughs. He hands me my package of meat. I take it. Our hands touch.

42

Glebe Cats

The first French word I learned was **Minou**, *and it remains attached to an elegant long-haired lady – who attracted every male around. Pets were seldom neutered then. One year we had thirteen cats in the house – three mothers and their litters, plus a tom – and practically populated the whole of the Glebe with Minou's descendants.*

As I cross the Bank Street bridge where it arches over the Canal, I can see the Parliament Buildings straight ahead. I'm on my way home from the library, which I've visited every week since I remember. It's frustrating that the limit is three books a time. I read them the first day. This Saturday, I have three thick Enid Blyton books in my arms. I take a shortcut through the Ex, anxious to get home and read.

I turn down my street, and Gentleman Jim walks towards me, tail up, and wraps himself around my legs. I bend to stroke him. You can see no more than a whisper of Minou in him: just his longish, soft coat. As happens every spring, he's been away for several days, and only came back filthy and ragged two nights ago. Most of the time since he's spent grooming himself, or sleeping it off in "his" chair – at least that's where I find him when I come back from school or errands – and his magnificent suit of black and white, with its lion-like ruff, is meticulously clean. Whenever I settle somewhere, sleeping or sitting or lying on my bed reading, he purrs and jumps up to join me. Years later, I'll write a tribute to him and to the arrogance of all cats that begins,

The cat's chair – is mine!

These white hairs – see?
are meant to dissuade you
from presumptuous settlement...

and goes on,

O sweet familiar cushion,
O lap that mocks the human,
swells with musk and sighs...

I'm looking forward to a Saturday afternoon that's perfect: new books, my favourite cat beside me, no little kids to look after.

I open the door quietly, drop my outer clothes, grab an apple and piece of cheese from lunch leftovers on the table, and slip upstairs, hoping to avoid any tasks my mother might suddenly discover for me to do. Gentleman Jim has disappeared, perhaps to the kitchen and his food bowl; I leave the bedroom door propped open to a cat width, as always. Someone's crying downstairs, but I hear Mom's voice, so don't go down.

Within minutes I'm deep in *The Valley of Adventure*, tracking a devilish villain through the underbrush with adventurous Jack and clever Philip and thoughtful Dinah and gentle Lucy-Ann. They've just landed in an airplane on a tiny unmarked landing strip and the pilot has taken off leaving them in the bush –

What's all that noise in the hall? I shut my ears more tightly, something I've learned to do in this house full of people. Jack has a plan, he's pulling off the rope he always carries wrapped around his waist –

"Sue, Mom says you have to come down," My brother is bothering me.

"Okay, just a minute." I go back to the cave full of unexplained canned supplies. But how can they open them without a can opener? Wait, Lucy-Ann has something in her pocket, a spoon left over from lunch, maybe if they sharpen it on a rock –

Another brother. "Mom says come down right now!"

"Just a sec, I'm coming." But how can they do that? They have to find some kind of flint or hard rock, maybe on the beach.

My little sister now, she seems to be the one who was crying. "Sue, you've got to come."

"Okay, okay!" I finish the last paragraph of the chapter, put my book face down on the bed. As I jump down the stairs two at a time, I see a man outside the door sliding a metal cage into a white van with letters on the side. I run across the hall. He starts the motor and drives away. My mother turns.

"Oh Susie, you're too late!"

"Too late for what?" My heart is pounding from more than jumping downstairs.

"Gentleman Jim has something wrong with him," she tells me, "a cat flu he picked on the streets. It's highly contagious and can't be cured. The man has just taken him off in the van to the Humane Society. They have to put him down." Kill him.

"But – I didn't even have a chance to see him, I didn't have a chance to say goodbye!"

"I know, honey, we tried to get you to come down before he left – "

O sturdy back to shield me
from intrusions or surprises,
O arms to wrap my rumble . . .

That day, at the age of ten, I decided that no books, no words would ever take precedence over someone I love. That never again would I absent myself from what was happening around me. Years later, Gentleman Jim made it impossible for me to leave my husband and children and escape to a Parisian garret to be a writer. Gentleman Jim determined that I'm always juggling what I owe to my writing with what I owe to those I love. This is a common dilemma, of course, in every field and every life. For me, it's symbolized by a white van driving away.

46

For an hour or a minute,
be weighted, be warmed –

rest small in my peace.

Ottawa Little Theatre

The Ottawa Little Theatre was a church before it was converted in 1913. When I was taking drama there in the early sixties at the age of 12 and 13, its hush and dust and old wood still echoed that gothic past, adding to the thrill. Recent renovations have made it more comfortable – but I remember what lies beneath.

Just past Ogilvy's department store, where my friends and I will have chips and gravy in the basement later, the number 1 bus stops, and I climb down into sharp October sunshine. An ornate limestone façade leans over my head, arched brows and heavy stone eyes half shut in weekend sleep – but willing to wink open for a moment to let me in. Ignoring the main doors, I turn to a side entrance that seems to glitter, so eager am I to enter. This is the gate to the drama classes that light my week. The classes are led by real actors. I can tell by their drawling voices, confident shoulders, amused curve of lip, sideways eye. Joe O'Brien is straight and arched, with strong, neat legs; Michelle Savage is draped in silky fabric and shakes a roar of glorious hair. I'm in love with them both. And with the other teenagers who gather each week from schools across Ottawa. The rehearsal stage downstairs, where we do our skits and exercises, is plywood sheets and two-by-fours nailed together and painted black. Spotlights, trained on the stage, throw the corners of the room into shadow.

Today is special, and I'm wound like a spring.

Joe gives us our instructions. We're to form groups and make up a skit involving a bench, someone asleep. Then, we're going upstairs.

I already know who my partners will be. We move to a dim corner, where stacks of flats painted like bushes and houses, and hats and wigs and dresses crammed onto racks, let us imagine ourselves as real actors, rehearsing for a real play. Rod's got a plot, Gwen's added a twist, Ellen's sketched out the dialogue, and Peter's thought of a trick ending. I'm the one on the bench. My job is to sleep, wake up, and gasp. Perfect. I'm coming to the conclusion that I'm not very good at this, though I desperately want to be. The skit seems easy in the dark, stone-smelling corner away from the lights. Just like my cellar at home, damp and a bit whispery.

We head upstairs. The doors, covered with puffy grey leather, swing open into a hall much bigger than our school auditorium. I take classes each Saturday, but have never attended a play; that's what parents do. Daylight streams in from somewhere high, and I look around at our small, untidy group, diminished in the echoing space.

It's all very well, playing at being actors in the dim below, but here we're in the light. The stage, sloped and polished and higher than my head, has heavy red curtains looped back to either side and drapes of black cloth; it seems huge and bare. In the cool, Saturday morning light, it's impossible to imagine myself up there.

The first group clatters up the side steps and mumbles through its skit.

"No, you must fill the theatre, you must reach out to the back rows!" Joe's own voice rings without effort through the empty tiers.

Another group. Another. I'm breathing in gulps.

And then it's our turn. I'll bump into things, make mistakes.

"Susan? Aren't you in this group? Go on up now."

Suddenly it seems like school.

"Get into position, I'll count three, then start."

The bench is just a few boards nailed together. What if it collapses? I ease myself down onto my side. Where do I put my head, my arms are in the way, my hip sticks up, what if my shirt gapes open? I've got to do something, so I shift an elbow under my head, turn my face into the bench so I can't see the watchers, and drop one knee across to bring my hip down. I'm trembling with the effort of staying still.

"One, two, three –"

The skit ends. I pretend to wake up, gasp, look surprised. There's a thin patter of clapping. As I rise, Joe calls out, "No, stay there. Lie down again. Now look, everyone, see how well she does that? Just plops herself down without any fuss, perfectly comfortable and natural, that's what I want from all of you, that's how to do it."

He nods at me. I sit up, flushed. He likes the way I lie down. I know how to be natural! That's what he wants us to do.

For a second on that stage, I can feel ghosts around me, applauding in the shadows. You're one of us, they say, one of the real actors who's walked these boards before. You know how to lie down on a rickety pretend bench. You can fill the Ottawa Little Theatre, satisfy all those seats, with your excellent relaxation. The sun chooses that moment to shine a bright yellow bar across the stage, my legs, my face. I rise to my feet, giddily, knees hardly shaking. Smile into the light.

Of us all, only Peter Blais went on to make a career as a professional actor, director, and producer. He and his partner Tom Alway now live in Nova Scotia near our summer house. As for myself, I learned, partially from experiences like the above, and partially through teaching drama classes to children at Ottawa community centres for that same Joe O'Brien, that what I can do on stage is be myself.

Lisgar Collegiate

Some teachers greeted us with "Don't think you're special just because you're accelerated." Walter Mann, Head of English for forty years at Lisgar Collegiate, just took advantage.

"How do you write?" he demands at our first class. This isn't a question I've ever considered. Usually teachers tell you, and you just go ahead and do it, you don't think about it.

"Well?" Dark eyes sparkling under beetling brows (the first time I've ever seen those, except in a book), hands on hips, he practically leaps around the classroom on energetic toes.

The smart boy in the class puts up his hand. "Um, well, you write an outline, and then…"

"No, no, no!"

The smart girl tries next.

"Well, um, if it's a story and not an essay, you, like, figure out who your characters are…"

"No, again, no, completely the wrong approach!"

We stare at him, a group of clever talkers, stymied. Not understanding, for once, what the teacher wants.

Suddenly he beetles in on me. "And you" – he glances at the class list – "Miss McClure? What do you think?"

I hate hearing my name out loud. Darn, he probably knows my parents, who also work for the NDP and are also teachers.

"Well?"

"Uh, well, I guess first you get some paper, and a pen." Pretty feeble.

"Aha, now we're getting somewhere!" Really?

"And then what? You, sir."

He points to the class clown.

"Hah, well, I guess you just put the pen on the paper and let loose. Sir."

A small ripple runs through the room. Hardly a laugh, more a breath out.

"Indeed you do. You, sir, to my surprise, may be smarter than you look!"

Another ripple. It's not easy to catch the full attention of this rather self-satisfied group.

Mr. Mann goes on to tell us, with many gestures, bounces, and barks of laughter and words, that our job as writers is not to think, not to plan, not to go through all the steps we've so punctiliously learned in twelve years of schooling. That comes later. The first job, the job of the real writer – and by now, we all want to be real writers – is to vomit.

"Vomit out your words. Spill them all over the page. Just empty your guts of every single thing that's in you to say about whatever you're writing about. Throw it up, get it out!"

Vomit? Throw up your guts? What kind of teacher is this?

Then, and only then, he tells us, do you apply the critical faculty to the task of moulding that pile of mess into something useful and beautiful.

All fall since then, he's been pushing us constantly to think differently, come up with another answer, pile on the speculation and imagination and hold forth as he does in a jousting rant of engaged intelligence.

We're studying *Lord of the Flies.* I'm excited by it, appalled by it. Great, he says, write me an essay, tell me how the novel gets into your guts. Usually, I receive nineties for work I think is trivial. This time, I've written far into the night, read and re-read and re-written again. Today, we're to receive our essays back.

"So," says Mr. Mann, entering at his quick trot with a sheaf of papers in hand. "Not a bad first effort for most of you."

He doesn't mean me. Mine is beyond a first effort.

"A few still don't seem to get the point. Too tight, too structured, too organized, without the necessary spark of imagination." His eyes rove over the class, lighting nowhere.

Definitely not me.

"And a couple of first-rate pieces. Essays that are pulled together, but full of verve. Two papers in the nineties. Well done."

Me? Again his eyes scan the class without alighting. Surely he must mean me?

"I'll pass them out alphabetically."

M is in the middle. Giggles and whispers on every side. A few faces concentrated sharply downward. The class clown folds his paper in half, spreads his fingers over it. Behind me, Fiona gasps, then taps me on the shoulder. "Sue, look, I can't believe it," she whispers. I turn around. Ninety-one per cent. That leaves only one paper to go.

"Miss McClure."

English is last class in the morning. I head quickly out the door and down to the bushes by the side of the Canal, walk all the way to the Pretoria Bridge to a willow tree I know. Make it back to the school just as the bell rings.

By the end of the afternoon, I know I can't go straight home. Certainly not with Fiona, my best friend, who's been trying to catch me alone all afternoon. I do something I've never done before: take my essay from my locker, and walk down the hall to the English room.

"Mr. Mann?" He's still there, writing on the blackboard. Turns towards me, those eyebrows arching up. I hold out the essay. "I don't understand."

He glances at it. "Seventy-two per cent? That's not bad, quite good in fact. What's worrying you?"

I look at him. This is not the bombastic voice of the daily harangue. He's really not much taller than I am, I suddenly notice, as he reaches to take the paper from my hand. His eyes are gentle, no mockery dancing in them, his voice low. No-one in the hall could possibly hear.

"What did I do wrong? How can I fix it?" Suddenly I can't speak.

"Ah. Well. Now. Now, that's a *good* question."

It's only twenty minutes maybe, out of a whole teaching career for him, and out of, eventually, twenty years in school for me. I pull up a chair, and he goes through the paper word by word, pointing out where I've made a point but left it undeveloped, leaping on typos and grammatical ambiguities, refining the opening and clarifying the ending. The approach is correct, he tells me. I have indeed poured out all my ideas on the page. This means there is something to work with. The rest is easy, just a matter of learning techniques. Here – here – and here, see how the metaphor is mixed up, how the language doesn't support the image? But if we just change this word…

That afternoon, I learn how to edit, the skill that has become my life's paid work. I learn that having the courage to spill your guts, and then the tenacity to face the raw mess and clean it up, is the essence of writing. I learn that the teacher who cares cannot be replaced.

When I bring the revised essay back, he tells me that he can't change my mark, "because I didn't give that chance to the rest of the class. However, don't worry."

My Christmas mark is A. By the end of the year, it's A-plus, and Mr. Mann has asked my permission to publish the essay in the school yearbook. And I'm writing poems.

When I took creative writing in Edmonton from W.O. Mitchell seven years later, in 1972, he proposed an approach he called "free flow." Write, he said, without censoring yourself. Ignore the internal critic, spill all the words onto the page and only then start looking for gems among the dross. Wait a second, I thought, that sounds familiar.

There are other memories of Lisgar: the Latin teacher with the horrendous breath, who nonetheless left me in love with Latin. The math teacher who failed me at Christmas, so that I got defiant eighties from then on and enrolled in a math class at Carleton, where I met my husband; Mrs. Todd was an unlikely Cupid. My embarrassing prom in the orange polka-dot dress. The predatory teacher who led the drama club.

I was at Lisgar in physics class when we heard John Kennedy was assassinated. The teacher told us, and no more knew what to say or do than we did.

Lisgar is still an impressive old stone building and still a top level academic high school. Three of my siblings, both my daughters, my niece, and my son-in-law, attended it. If I happen to pass by the school around noon on a spring day and see clumps of students lounging in a sleepy haze on the grass along the Canal, I half wish I were among them.

A few years ago, I found myself beside Walter Mann in an elevator at Carleton University, and tried to tell him what those twenty minutes meant to me. You gave me permission to write, I said, and showed me how to do it. I could see he didn't remember. It didn't matter. I had a chance to say thank you.

And if, on any given day when, faced with the white page or blank computer screen, I lose courage, I still conjure up Walter Mann, with his devilish grin and highly polished, dancing shoes, and tell myself to get on with it. Vomit it up. Cleaning up the mess, as he said, is the easy part.

Le Monde and Rasputin's Music Café

The sixties was the heyday of dangerous houses, exciting houses, houses where things happened.

In the last years of high school and the first years of university, 1963-67 or so, my real life is centred in coffee houses. Le Hibou, where I sat on the black floor as a child to listen to Pete Seeger, has moved to Sussex Drive, and I see acts there like Muddy Waters and Brownie McGee, and Tom Rush, who is just about the sexiest guy in the universe.

The place where I spend my time, though, is Le Monde, founded in the basement of St. George's Anglican Church on Metcalfe Street near Laurier Avenue by the minister, Pat Playfair. Le Monde, where I wear a fur skirt, argue the theology of hell, am bested for my one big theatre break by one of my closest friends (a salutary lesson in the world of high culture), hear some of the best music available then and now, and witness a tangle with the Satan's Choice that ends in court.

My parents are overwhelmingly busy with other children, who are mixed up with sixties drugs among other problems. I've always been the "good girl," and they're right, I do stay away from the drugs and the philosophy of dropping out. There's only so far a Quaker girl can travel from her sense of responsibility and guilt.

They discount the dangers of unsupervised teenage libido, however. When the strains of juggling up to four boyfriends at a time, some of whom take their turn being nasty to me, becomes too much, I try to kill myself with an Aspirin overdose. After a period of intense supervision and recovery, Le Monde is the only place my parents feel they can leave me for an evening, safe in a church with others my age. They're right, but not for those reasons.

In fact, the reason I don't get tangled up in the seamier aspects of coffeehouse culture is the manager of Le Monde, Russ Barton. He's a confident, smart, very funny Englishman of twenty-five years of age – an old man. But with a soft heart and a lot of common sense. When I find an excuse to visit his apartment behind the church one day (returning a book, I think), and back him into his own closet in a way that requires him to kiss me or throw me out, he overcomes his qualms about dating a young thing of only sixteen. His own sense of responsibility and guilt, however, demands that I be protected from the excesses of sex, drugs, and rock 'n roll that are the norm in some circles in the sixties, so I get the pleasure of being girlfriend to the Top Dog while suffering none of the perils of the environment Russ lives in daily. For example, we don't drink together.

Russ and I remained friends, even after Ian came into my life and artist Susan Feindel into his. We now all enjoy nostalgic evenings together (in Nova Scotia, where they, too, now live. What does this mean?). Russ is still confident, smart, and funny, but somehow he doesn't seem nearly as old to me any more.

Like Le Hibou, however, Le Monde is long gone, as is the Wasteland, which hosted poetry readings before they became common. SAW Gallery, then on Rideau, is still around. That's where I met John Tappin, the artist who later covered my naked torso with plaster body casts. SAW still stages wild events in black rooms at Arts Court; I've read and performed there with my two music-and-poetry groups, SugarBeat and Geode.

The spiritual successor to Le Monde is Rasputin's Music Café. For almost 30 years, Dean Verger has hosted an eclectic, vibrant series of musical and creative events, first with his mother Helen and now with Ruth, a story teller and performer and his life-partner.

SugarBeat's first 15-minute show was held there, at Dean's Wednesday Open Stage, as were a number of our full-evening events. It's where we launched the *SugarBeat* CD, the *Geode* CD, and the *Until the Light Bends* book and CD. It's where I gave a reading and Mary Tougas, an artist from Gabriola Island (and mother of my riding friend Nancy Binnie), showed a series of paintings based on my poems. It's where Geode held a music-and-poetry improv session for Ottawa poets like Nadine McInnis and Sandra Nicholls. Every acoustic musician who comes through town ends up in Rasputin's at some point. The Ottawa Folk Festival holds its meetings there. The songwriters gather there, the Celtic group, the old-time group, the Jamalongs. Like its owner, like its historic precedent, Rasputin's is infinitely flexible, curious, welcoming, and, under the big smile, stringent. Another story just waiting to be told.

Carleton University

I wanted to drop Grade 13, do anything else instead. I made up a plan for independent study. My father suggested I skip the grade and head straight to qualifying year at Carleton University. Flickers of memory remain from the next four years.

– Bouncing down the tunnel under the Quad, full of pure joy because I'm wearing jeans and reading a book by Emily Dickinson and my first class tomorrow is at 2 pm so I can sleep in.

– Professor Trevor Tolley reading John Donne's "I wonder by my troth, what thou, and I / Did, till we loved?" so intently, and beautifully, that he and we are in tears. Sometimes he forgets to teach *about* the poetry because he so much wants to read us more.

– Enrolling in the first course on Canadian literature ever taught at Carleton. Imagine, no Canlit before 1967! We'll be using a solemn hardcover tome, which I still have, buried somewhere.

– Professor James Downey's brilliant lectures on Modern British literature. The Beatles don't thrill me; this level of erudition does. The student party at which, just barely, we both remember we're student and teacher, and both married, besides.

– The French professor who proves there are drama teachers everywhere.

– John Baglow, then the editor of the student paper, *The Charlatan*, rejecting my first submission. The poem is mostly about my belly, if I recall correctly.

– Meeting Ian in Math 101. By now, Russ has gone west to work for the Company of Young Canadians. Ian is the teaching assistant for one section of this large televised course. As he chalks his name on the board the first day – Mr. McMaster – I determine to never call him that and remain mum until I discover his first name. He notices my boots – ankle-high, with a buckle – and when I drop a pencil on the floor, gallantly picks it up.

Ian, as I discover he's called when I stop him after class and ask, is tall and wears cowboy boots and has floppy dark brown hair. For the next two weeks I time my departure from class to coincide with his, and bump into him at the snack machines. "I don't understand calculus" turns out to be the effective line.

Carleton was everything to me a university should be. I met smart people and foolish people, had adventures and disappointments, read hundreds of books and wrote scores of papers and exams, and left with a sigh of relief. I like to do things, not research them, and hate deadlines unless I've set them myself.

When I graduated in 1970 with a B.A., I spent two months as a bank clerk at the salary level of $2,500 per year. Ottawa Teachers' College was free, and the course only one year long. I didn't want to be a teacher – I'd taken care of too many children in my life – but it was better than the bank. I graduated with an Elementary Teacher's Certificate for Ontario in 1971, taking top place in academics and second place in practice teaching. The Principal had called me to his office beforehand to say I really should attend the graduation dance (where the awards would be handed out), but I had no formal gown. I wore my wedding dress, with the sleeves cut out.

A Quaker Wedding

I got married at eighteen. My friends tried to discourage me. Why don't you just live together? they asked.

It's 5 July 1969, and ours is the first Quaker wedding in Ottawa. I look around the lovely wood-lined hall of the old church that has recently replaced the rooms the Meeting rented at the YMCA. So I'm only eighteen, I think, but Ian is twenty-three after all. And my parents were both nineteen when they got married. Practically a family tradition!

The room is full of daisies, from Enid Frankton's garden; she's the mother of my best friend, Gwen. Enid's blooms are large, beautiful, meticulously white. This morning my sisters and I also picked daisies in the fields south of Ottawa to decorate for the wedding; guests sitting near those more straggly bouquets will brush ants out of their clothes for days. The hall is never used for our small group of thirty or so worshippers on Sunday, but it's needed for the more than a hundred family, friends, and Friends who are already arriving. I'm wearing a yellow cotton shift covered with embroidered white lawn and tied with a velvet ribbon, made by Sarah Pouliot of Sarah Clothes. It's the only dress I've ever had made to order.

Ian appears wearing a blue tropical seersucker suit and white shoes, which is what he thinks an elegant groom in a summer wedding should wear. It's an era of embroidered jeans and Edwardian suits with skin-tight trousers, and handsome as Ian is, I almost switch grooms and grab his brother Jim instead: at least he has sideburns! Unfortunately, Jim is already engaged to Marie.

Ian and I take our places at the front of the hall, and silence falls. A few people speak into the quiet worship. When the time feels right, we stand and make our declarations to each other. Then we exchange rings, bands of gold wire woven by John Tappin, and kiss. I'm so flustered I mistakenly put the ring on Ian's right hand; later my grandmother asks if this is a Quaker custom. Poet George Johnston recites "To the marriage of true minds" and forgets the words halfway through and has to sit down. (This has left me with a particular fondness for the poem, so I take his blessing as read.) Several others stand and add their thoughts. Everyone shakes hands, and then we all sign the large parchment wedding certificate prepared and lettered by my father.

Ian's mother, Nancy, cuts pieces from a cake covered with icing daisies. She took a cake decorating course, and wanted to do a lovely three-tier extravaganza, but I insisted on a large flat cake. Next time, I'll tell her to go ahead. Then we all traipse back to the large house on Broadway that my family is renting this year, for a three-day reception and party.

Unfortunately, as bride and groom, we have to leave before the cake is even gone.

My family moved to Ottawa from Toronto when I was five partly to help establish a Meeting of the Religious Society of Friends (Quakers) that could lobby the federal government. Being raised a Quaker had benefits and consequences. I met poet George Johnston through Quakers; his response to my early poems, all purpose but true (I've used it often myself, since), was "you do have to find your own voice," and "If you are going to write poetry, nothing will stop you." I also met poet Elizabeth Brewster through Quakers, and her remark that "you have developed into a genuine poet" has sustained me over years.

My childhood was full of peace marches, ban the bomb marches, and protest marches, my values were shaped by principles of community, and respect for "the light in every person," my approach to decision-making was modelled on Quaker ideas of "the sense of the meeting" – a flexible form of consensus. This orientation led me to organize all my projects, starting with *Branching Out*, using a consensual model, and pushed me to find ways to integrate my poetry with peace-making activities: pacifism not passivism.

In time, the old wooden building was renovated into two townhouses, plus a new Meeting room and offices. You can still see the shape of the peaked entrance at 91 Fourth Avenue, or enter through the porch on the east side to worship with Quakers in what is now a gathering almost too large for the space.

To celebrate our thirtieth wedding anniversary, we retraced a route we'd travelled the summer before the wedding – but in the easy direction. Early First Drafters Ruth Pinco (also a Quaker) and her partner David Peebles came with us; Ruth had been on the original trip. This time, we canoed from the Big Rideau Lakes all the way down the Rideau River, following both wind and current and eating at restaurants and staying in hotels, arriving after five days at the foot of our street and carrying the canoe on our heads to the house. Our daughters had made us a party, and friends were spilling out of the house to greet us. Seems we didn't make a mistake after all.

Sunnyside Avenue

*In 1975, after our sojourn in Edmonton, we returned to Ottawa and bought a row house on Sunnyside Avenue much like the ones I grew up in. I'd just read Virginia Woolf's essay "A Room of One's Own," which states that having a personal space is vital, so one room – the best room at the back – was mine, the first I'd had to myself since marriage. Unfortunately, there seems to be more to writing immortal poems than having a room to do it in. For a few months, I spent a lot of effort on organizing and decorating. I poked around the house, drafted articles for **Branching Out,** burned a lot of potatoes, bored myself with a journal, suffered through sudden exercise attacks.*

One night in November 1975, Ian and I go out for dinner to celebrate our new, settled lives, and to confirm, once and for all, that we will not have children. I've looked after too many kids in my life, and besides, we've been married for seven years and are having a fine time as we are. It's a romantic, glowing meal, mellow with golden candle light and our plans for a life of travel and freedom. As Ian drains the last of the wine into our glasses, and we raise them to our lips, he looks at me. I look at him. "Do you think… ," I say, "we'd be missing something…?" he finishes.

Our first daughter, Sarah Aven, is conceived that night, I am absolutely sure. John Tappin, our sculptor friend, is now living next door. As prospective godfather, he suggests a unique way to celebrate the pregnancy.

There's a wonderful store, Loretta's Bakery, on Bank between Fourth and Third Avenues, that makes crusty white loaves and hazelnut cream confections that have never been equalled in my experience. The latter are my reward, sustenance, and temptation to nausea through nine monthly sessions of body-casting during that first pregnancy. John has an art studio in Corpus Christi School at Fourth and Lyon, as part of a community arts program. Every month, I strip and slather the front half of my body with Vaseline from neck to thighs. Then John and Ian and friends quickly mix and smooth dental alginate all over me, holding it in place with plaster bandages.

By the time the cast sets, I'm usually sweating and nauseous. John pries it carefully off me, cutting it away from body hair, if necessary, with a long, flexible, and very sharp knife, and sets it into sand. From these negatives, he then produces nine plaster bodies, which eerily show every crease and freckle on my skin in hard antiseptic white.

These hang dustily around his studio for years, aging ghosts of a baby now thirty years old and a mother herself. He also carves some wonderful wooden pieces inspired by the castings – shoulders, a set of pregnant breasts – but his plan to do the whole series languishes for lack of funds.

Baby in Academe

So, even if I couldn't manage to write an immortal poem, I could at least inspire an artist. Not so bad. And anyway, by that time I was starting the journalism master's that was meant to teach me what I'd learned with **Branching Out.**

It's my second year of grad studies, 1976, and I have a three-week-old baby, Sarah Aven, named for the flower. I pack her in the carriage and take her to class, blatantly breastfeeding in proper feminist mode whenever she needs it and dropping bits of donut on her head as I eat lunch with her strapped in a Snugli around my waist.

That arrangement generates an article in the Citizen – "Baby in Academe" – and lasts three months. In the photo, I look completely exhausted; Aven is sleeping happily. I take the next term off, and head back to school only when she can go to the Carleton day care while I'm in class, Christopher Levenson's creative writing class, some of the time.

He's a good poet and good teacher, thoughtful, very knowledge-able, and I learn a lot about the history and techniques of poetry. As well, it gives me a reason and deadline to finish my poems. A spur to overcome the anxiety.

The class includes Dayv James French, who goes on to become a novelist and story writer; and Nancy Ross, who divorces her husband just as her short stories are getting really good and heads home to the States, where she marries an ophthalmologist and keeps publishing for some years anyway – we lose touch eventually. Dayv and Nancy and I meet for a couple of years as the Hopewell Writers' Group.

As well, Chris invites me and others to his Ottawa Poetry Group, which meets monthly. One remarkable evening we gather at Carol Shields' house on the Driveway, with George Johnston, among others. Try reading your student poem in that company. I also meet poets more at my stage in the OPG who become close friends, like Blaine Marchand, Nadine McInnis, Sandra Nicholls, John Barton. The story of that long-lived, seminal group has recently been told elsewhere.

Another member of Chris's class, annoying and inspiring at the same time, is Claire Harrison, a Classics scholar who gets the only A in the course while the rest of us receive A-minuses, and who does almost immediately become a professional writer. Of romances. Teaches her how to keep the reader turning pages, she tells me at a party a few years later, and besides, she makes a fine penny out them. How can I look down my nose at achievements we all strive for? She then does a CBC radio "Ideas" series on the romance and its place in society, which is almost a feminist polemic, dammit, and tops it off by having a "straight" novel published by McLelland and Stewart.

By the next year, I was involved in a gaggle of projects and publications, including helping Nancy as first editor of *Oscar* (the *Ottawa South Community Association Review*), sitting on the boards of poetry magazines *Quarry* and *Arc*, writing a column on local cultural events, running editing classes at the community centre and helping with the neighbourhood babysitting co-op. I looked at my date book the other day: at one point I was dividing my energy, in fifteen-minute chunks, among forty different projects. No wonder I ran off to play with First Draft.

Dow's Lake

Aven was such a joy that it seemed only sensible to have another child. The books we read all said that it was better to have two, though perhaps we chose the books to match our desires. Certainly Sylva Morel, born in February 1980, and named after a mushroom, was a different but equal delight.

We've just come under the Bronson Bridge, and emerged on Dow's Lake where the "world's longest ice rink" splits into two skateways, one to the boathouse where you can now change back into boots and drink hot chocolate, and the other around the corner to the locks. The tall and short and spindly and stout trees in the Arboretum line the north shore of the spur, all capped with slushy hats. It's been an irritating Christmas, with the weather see-sawing back and forth from wet to sudden freezing cold to thaw again. The Canal surface is a crisscross of blade marks and rough lumps of ice, frozen into a humpy mess.

At eight-and-a-half months pregnant, I'm walking. Aven, now just about three and a half, is attempting to stand on her first skates; she clings to Ian's and John's hands. John grew up mostly in the United States, and is shaky on his own blades, while Ian takes pleasure in making loops and skid-stops around my cautious progress whenever we go out together, even if I'm not pregnant. Just because he started out on hockey skates, while I was stuck still trying to conquer those "figure-skating" twirls.

Ian and Aven and John are about twenty feet away from me out on the ice. For safety, because I don't want to trip and trigger the baby's arrival in the middle of an ice rink, I'm sticking close to the cracked cement wall of the Canal. It looms a few feet above my head; the water is almost drained each year before the ice freezes, and skaters climb down sets of wooden steps put into place by National Capital Commission workers in late fall, so we're all down below the level of the surrounding parkland. I pick my way in my clumsy boots through the rough snow and ice piled just under the wall, while Aven and the men skate further out, where the ice is smoother.

"Ring-around-a-rosy, all fall down!" All three fall to the ice in a tangle of mittens and blades and laughter. The NCC first cleared the Canal for skating in 1970-71, I remember. Just a square rink on Dow's Lake to start with. Now the groomed surface is almost eight kilometres long; it reaches all the way from the National Arts Centre to Carleton University. And it's thronged, with almost a million skaters each year, so much like a Kurelek painting that it's almost embarrassing. Skating is one of those activities that will always be a mix of floating scarves and bright jackets and fuzzy hats and big smiles, I guess, no matter how fashions change. I shuffle, sliding on my boots, out of the way of a fast bundle of energy zipping by on tiny hockey skates. Even if he – she? – falls, there's almost nowhere to fall to. Oops, there the bundle goes, tipping up without a wail. Just gets up and skates off again. That's what we're hoping for our daughter, that soon she'll whip around on her own. Even if I can't do much, it's still a pleasure to be out here on this brilliant, windy, January day, and watching her take her first skating steps.

Keeping an eye on Aven and the men, I tread slowly and very carefully along the slippery mush of ice and snow at the side of the waterway. Unable to fit into my own gear, I'm wrapped in Ian's old

Army greatcoat over a thick sweater, and muffled with scarf, hat, mitts, and high boots to try to defeat the damp wind that blasts down the ice. It's stronger as we move from the shelter of the cement Canal walls onto the unprotected expanse of Dow's Lake.

Someone shrieks – a child who looks no more than five or six has broken through a patch of fragile surface ice to the thicker shell below. He's fallen down in the exposed pool, and icy water is soaking his snowsuit. I stop and turn, ready to help – oh it's all right, here comes the big sister – and suddenly, without a sound or tremor, I plunge down through the ice straight as a knife into a glass of iced tea.

I gasp, shocked. Water pours into my boots. Ice breaks around me. I reach for the bottom, the water is shallow here. Isn't it? All I have to do is put down my feet–

I'm still sinking. Now I'm past my waist. Frantically I kick my feet in boots which are heavier every second. I can't feel bottom. But I'm only a few feet from the shore!

The heavy wool coat billows up around me as frigid water rakes through layers of cloth to my skin. A current – a strong current! – pulls my feet sideways. I begin to tip up.

"Ian!" I shout, "Ian!!"

There must be something in my voice. Despite the noise of the crowds and the crying child nearby, despite the blast of wind and Aven's laughter, suddenly he's sliding towards me on his stomach.

John drops Aven on the ice – she squeals with fright – and grabs Ian's legs, throwing himself flat as well. I slip farther into the hole, still can't feel anything but icy water pushing me sideways. Where are the skate patrols, how can I possibly get out, what –

In a single heave, from flat on the ice, Ian grabs me under the arms and lifts me out, sopping coat and soaked boots and all.

Aven cries louder, tries to crawl with her skate-covered feet to where I am. John turns to her and Ian slides me farther onto safer ice, helps me roll onto my hands and knees. Then he takes off, zigzagging through the dense crowd, to warm up the car and bring it as close as possible to the Canal.

People emerge from the crowd to help, a skate patroller, a young man and his father, two teenage girls who pick up the dropped scarves and hats. John helps me up and gives me an arm, and then awkwardly hoists my daughter in his other arm. All around us children continue to play skate tag or practise twirls and skids. Mothers and fathers push sleds and call out. Couples stroke by in sedate tandem toward the hot chocolate at the far end of the lake. My eyelashes start to freeze. Wet hair whips my face in the wind.

And the wind is bitter now, blasts right at us. The two girls come along to carry things as we set off. It's farther than it looks to the car. In the distance, Ian bends forward as he races towards it, rather like the speed skaters we often see. Aven still gulps air, and I try to hug her without upsetting John's precarious balance.

Then run a quick internal check. No pains or even movement – the baby is quiet for once.

Just take it easy, I hear my mother's voice in my head. Go slowly, don't slip or fall, soon you'll be in a nice warm car.

I look down at the ice to make sure I don't stumble – and my heart jogs into my throat. The water dripping from my coat is red. Pale, just tinged with colour, but visible against the white ice. But I don't feel anything. Could shock make me numb?

We're still far from the car. Keep walking, don't say anything. John has more than enough to handle right now. If I do go into labour, right here and now, maybe the girls could take Aven while John calls an ambulance. But where's a phone? I'm not thinking clearly…

And there's Ian now. He drives right over the snow piled by the locks, then jumps out in his sock feet (later he tells me it was quicker than putting on his boots), and trots across the last few yards to help us into the car. The heater is blowing full blast. Red liquid still drips from my coat, but Ian doesn't say anything. Neither do I.

A quick U-turn onto Colonel By, gun it past the snow dump at Bronson, under the bridge we passed twenty minutes ago. Zoom around the fancy houses on the Canal with their outdoor Christmas trees still lit, coast through two stop signs and squeal left onto Sunnyside.

No room on the street in front of the house for the car – skaters fill all the spaces. Ian double-parks, lifts Aven out and pulls me squelching from the front seat. While he drives around back, John helps us inside and off with our coats. I drop mine on the floor, and head upstairs shedding clothes as I go. I fill a deep bath with hot water and bubbles and climb in. John sets up a chair just beyond the open bathroom door where he can see my face.

As I sink under the foam, Ian arrives with sweet hot tea. He changes Aven and himself into dry clothes, gives John a towel and a sweater, and we all sit, or in my case lounge under bubble bath, in the bathroom for a while, recovering.

Then Ian calls our family doctor, Jim Dickson, a wiry, humorous Scot who runs marathons. Also the city coroner. "Nothing to worry about, she's tough," he says. Which seems to be true. I still feel fine, no signs of labour coming on. Maybe the pink water was an optical illusion.

I turn on the hot tap with my toe, and sink further down, while the others brew more tea and cut sandwiches. It's been an afternoon to make a person hungry.

Finally, full and satisfied with what he can see of me under the bubbles, Ian goes off to pick up the sodden clothes shed in the front hall as we came in.

"So that's what happened to my red felt pen," he says, coming up the stairs. "It's dripped red all over my coat and the floor. What a mess."

"What?" I say.

"What?" says John.

We look at each other.

"I didn't want to say anything."

"I didn't want to worry you."

"What are you talking about?" asks Ian.

Not until three in the morning do I wake up with the shakes, unable to dislodge the image, not of me, but of my daughter, slipping through the ice, feeling it break around her and soak her snowsuit, her boots, my daughter who doesn't know how to kick, who gets pulled under the ice as I run towards her, who is grabbed out of my hands by the current that I can still feel dragging at my legs.

But then, it didn't happen that way, did it?

Blackout
by Ian McMaster

> *Some stories are so much a part of family history that it seems you were there yourself. Ian's Dow's Lake tale is about bicycling home after a party during the blackout of 2003 that closed down most of the east coast.*

The night is moonless, so dark I can see only to the edge of the light cast by my headlamp. As I wobble slowly along the boardwalk around Dow's Lake, nearly running into a rabbit, I begin to hear voices ahead. Voices of a decidedly boisterous and youthful variety. Hmm. My pulse quickens, as a knot of people – perhaps a dozen twenty-somethings – break into my bubble of light.

"Sir!" one calls out, "Can you help us?"

What do they want? My wallet? My bike? Directions to the beer store?

A burly youth with a beer in his hand steps closer. "Sir, do you know the words to 'The Log Driver's Waltz'?"

Now there are quite a few Ottawans who would recognize the song, but, I expect, not many who know all the words. I look the young man in the eye, strike a pose, and began to sing: *"If you ask any girl in the parish round here…"*

Eyes widen in surprise, and they begin to grin.

"I do like to waltz with a log driver…" As I hit the first chorus a couple of voices join me.

"For he goes burlin' down, and down white water… " I finish with a flourish, and bow to the whoops and applause of what turns out to be Carleton students partying in the park because the residence lights

are out. I tell them that, right where we are standing, J.R. Booth once had a lumber mill that processed the white pine cut by the loggers in the song, up to half a billion board feet a year. As I bike off, my spinal hairs still tingle – but now with a visceral sense of connection between those long-ago workers, the students, and myself.

"If you ask anyone, from the valley around…"

Meeting to Remember

Stillness is at the heart
(still, still the heart)

It's 1982. I'm sitting quietly in the Meeting Room of the old wooden building on Fourth Avenue where Friends gather, at the core of Quakerism, in silent worship and remembrance of Friend and family friend Len Huggard. In a Meeting for Worship there's no minister or set readings. A person who feels moved by the Light stands to speak, then sits down into silence again. A good, centred Meeting is mostly silent, with a few words here and there.

This is a centred Meeting. Too centred for me. The children have left – they stay for a few minutes at the beginning of the hour, then slip off to First Day School with a parent. Not my turn today. Undistracted now, the forty or so adults left behind lean back into their chairs, hands and ankles folded or still at their sides, eyes hooded or closed. Under the white noise of lights and air, there's a hair-raising pulse, almost as if we are all breathing together. I can feel myself beginning to tremble.

The nickname "Quakers" for the Religious Society of Friends came from the tendency of Friends to shake with the intensity of the words of God coming through. I've felt this twice before. My guts are moving all by themselves, and my breath, so calm seconds before, is quickening to a pant. If I don't get up soon, I'll be incoherent and stuttering. No-one else has spoken yet. I don't want it to be me.

"There is a stillness at the heart of things…"

The words pull me to my feet, unplanned, unrehearsed. A

few words, in immaculate order, not my doing. The Light shining through, filling me to my core, drilling through to my skeleton. I don't remember the other words. I fumble for the chair behind me.

And now I really tremble. As if I'm in the path of a sharp cold mountain wind with no coat. I left it too long, the reaction is too great. I may not be able to stay here, still in my chair. I look up, look around, nausea rising in my throat – and unbelievably, incredibly, my five-year-old daughter Aven is at the door. Aven, who never, ever, causes trouble or doesn't do what's expected of her. Aven, I was told later, who refused to stay in First Day School and insisted on coming to see her mom, would not be put off, would not wait until Meeting was over.

Aven walks right across the room and pulls herself onto my lap. Leans back against my chest, tucks her head under my chin. Sticks her thumb in her mouth. I wrap my arms around her, feel heat opening inside me like a bowl of soup, wrapping me like a blanket warmed in the dryer, close my eyes as all the tension and shakes drain away.

Dear God, I think. Dear God, who brings my daughter to me when I need her.

I went home and wrote down as much as I could remember of those words, which I won't call mine; this became a wordmusic piece that I performed many times with First Draft, "Death of a youngish man." What started as a moment in a memorial for a particular person, became, by the alchemy of poetry, a lens through which I remember many friends, and every detail of that day.

at the heart
        still here
                sleep
                        still
                              silence

National Gallery of Canada

In 1988, we moved from Sunnyside to Belmont Avenue, and gained a substantial mortgage. I began to work full time for the government in various departments. Colin had me stand in for him twice at Labour Canada while he took writing breaks; Liette Vinet-Venne, who was his manager, taught me copy editing from the ground up. I was at Investment Canada when a chance came up to apply for a job that sounded made for me.

As I struggle through the heavy circular glass doors in the staff wing of the National Gallery of Canada, with my arms full of publications I've written or edited – poetry books, literary and art magazines, wordmusic books that interleave scores with art plates and poems – I think how quiet it is in here. How, wandering through a room full of paintings from time to time before settling to quietly untangle a text would be just about ideal.

The position is editor of art catalogues in the National Gallery's Publications division, and the first step is an editing test three hours long. It's tough. I love it. Irene Lillico, the administrator (who will become my best Gallery friend), tells me they'll be in touch. I'm not prepared to wait. As I head down the corridor to the door, I dump my books on the desk of Serge Thériault, the Chief of Publications, and tell him firmly, "I'm a poet who works with artists. I belong here – this is my home."

He laughs but wave his hands. "Non, non, it's all right, you don't have to leave those – "

It's too late, I have no time to listen. My father-in-law is at the Civic hospital, dying of cancer, and it's my turn to sit with him. Even making it here today was difficult, and the knit skirt and sweater I threw on had to pass for interview clothes because I had neither energy nor time to find anything else. But after seeing the kind of work I'd do, meeting the man I'd do it for, I'm lighthearted for the first time in weeks, bouncy as I hurry down the corridor. Yes, this is where I want to be – surely he'll see that?

And indeed he does.

I join the staff on 4 January 1989. The Gallery becomes my haven. Within weeks, I find the rhythm of the place, a rhythm that lets me gaze out at the Ottawa River flowing past beyond my office, and, if it's been a good day with lots done, occasionally write a small poem.

> *May flies flicker against salt-stained glass,*
> *obtrude on my view of the far-off hills,*
> *so fine in their glistening coats of green...*

My office window, on the windy side of the building and three full-length panes wide, is (I discover) the place we all gather to watch the weather pouring in. Some evenings, especially in the depths of winter, I stay late, hoping to out-wait the storm, or at least avoid the jammed streets that would hem me in for a good half-hour on Mackenzie, the only road out of here.

> *Outside my office window*
> *flocks of black starlings*
> *fall from roof and chimney,*
> *cross flocks of white flakes...*

Civil Service

Only two years and twelve days passed before my haven was invaded.

The CBC wakes me through a haze of birds and sun. Canada – at war – news I never thought to hear, locked in our civil playground behind the linked fences of money and seas.

I walk to my office through the main building of the Gallery, hoping to calm myself within its high halls and soft greys and browns, with the sun pouring through the glass panes. Climb slowly up the long ramp to the Great Hall, as slowly as the Karen Jamieson dancers imitating mountain climbers conquering heights in a performance I saw there once, and pause to look across the river to the cliffs, where the Peace Tower rises straight as a contradiction and the Parliamentary Library sits round and serene as a perfumed matron.

If I could, I wouldn't be here today. Would renounce entirely the government that has taken us into a war – the first Canadian war of my life – and for such a cynical reason: to support Britain and the United States in a bid to protect American oil resources in the Persian Gulf.

But I'm part of that government. I'm a citizen of Canada. Now, for the first time in a long freelance career, I'm also a civil servant. What my government does is done by me.

I turn from the sight of Parliament floating over the Ottawa River, move more quickly through the second corridor towards the staff building that lies beyond the cafeteria. Bright artworks by children hang along the way.

It's Thursday morning, and time for our regular staff meeting –

twelve of us together in a quiet, sunny room, around a polished table of honey-coloured wood. The Gallery is in the middle of a political controversy about whether a dress sewn of slabs of raw meat and a hoop skirt made of live electric wires are works of art. Are we wasting taxpayers' money? Shouldn't we use the steaks to feed the hungry? *States of Being*, an exhibition by Jana Sterbak, opens in two months, and we're in the last stages of preparing the exhibition catalogue.

Today we're supposed to be discussing how best to present the bed of heated wire spikes, the dress of bloody meat, the electrified skirt. Sterbak is known. Even before the show opens, rumours of these pieces are generating outrage. What angle will we take in the catalogue to support the artist without courting sensationalism?

"The curator suggests – " Serge begins to speak.

I can't seem to concentrate, keep dripping small tears.

safe from harm and harmless
as I'd hoped we were

The CBC intro tag for the news begins on a radio in the office next door. Serge falters, and we all shift in our seats.

"I'll get it." The production manager brings back the radio and turns it up. We're sending 4500 soldiers – civil servants – people – to the Gulf. Two destroyers, and a supply ship. Maybe fighter planes, as well.

The words charge my body with a buzz of angry sparks. I push past a chair, stumble into the hall. I want to storm the Hill, throw my body on the runways – but there are projects on my desk, my children expect me home –

protector or protected?

Anyway, what difference can I make, with connections as weak as mine?

responsive and responsible
as I'd thought we were

The surge to flight or protest, flickers, grounds. I return with a mug of coffee as hot as I can bear it. My co-workers hardly notice; faces wired to the radio, they move their chairs automatically to let me in.

The production man nods and crosses his arms as the broadcast ends. "We'll teach them," he says. I suppress the urge to respond; I'm afraid I'll start to shout, or cry.

An editor chews his lip; he's come back not too long ago from a trip to the near east, where he has relatives and friends.

The silence lasts too long – none of us knows quite what to say. We weathered the Quebec Referendum by carefully not speaking about it, except quietly, person to person. Our habit is reserve on all political matters. When something difficult does come up, we pass it off with a joke. Serge coughs, picks up a sheet of paper.

"I received a memo this morning. There are new security measures as of today, new guards in the halls, and at the doors."

"Yes, but what *about* those guards," a co-worker mutters to me. "A lot of them come from over there. Shouldn't we be watching them?"

I'm too taken aback to reply.

"... so report anyone you see in the halls that you don't know personally. Ask if you can help, ask why they are there. We're not really expecting bombs, but this is a high profile federal institution, and we must be prepared."

I leave the room to fill my cup again. The coffee, stewing since eight o'clock, is hot, acrid, strong. I stir in sugar, the first time in ten years. Then another spoonful. Return to my seat.

And slowly, we lean our elbows on the smooth, light wood. Slowly resume our talk of strategies and deadlines, efficiencies and costs. Twelve civil, public servants together around a table.

no thirteenth one to blame
in this saintless room

Later, back in my office, I light a small candle and set it on the window sill, in defiance of fire regulations. Serge says, only, please blow it out when you leave.

I burn a candle every day for the length of the war.

States of Being opened on 8 March 1991, a week after the war ended. At the opening, a model wore the meat dress. There were two live performances during the exhibition, as well, "Remote Control," with a dancer operating the electrified skirt from a harness inside, and "Artist as a Combustible," in which a dish of gunpowder attached to the artist's head was ignited. These performances were staged in the Great Hall against the backdrop of Parliament Hill, seen through the glass.

Belmont Avenue

Altogether, it was a miserable winter, the winter of 1997-98. Heavy snows, cold snaps, whining wet winds. After Christmas, the weather turned violent in the worst ice storm I'd known. Freezing rain fell for days in a row. Trees cracked and broke, wires snapped, power went off in hundreds of thousands of households across Ontario and Quebec. The maple sugar industry took the hardest hit, perhaps, financially, but many other businesses from farming to construction were affected. Forests and woodlands and parks were ravaged. And even poets couldn't just huddle inside with their words.

With a crash not a whimper...

Another clump of ice slips off a broken branch as Ronnie edges the car underneath, and drops with a sound like breaking glass onto the hood. The ice coats the twigs and wires and sidewalks, and even the Christmas tinsel still wrapped around porch railings, like the touch of the Ice Queen, like the Viking sagas, like the End of the World.

We slide our way in the low-slung car around fallen branches, shatters of broken ice, trees that crack above us as we pass under the weight of a crystal sheet that is almost one, full, unbelievable, inch thick. As unbelievable as the time the river flooded the street and we paddled up and down it in canoes – but colder.

Ronnie and I are together braving a storm that has lasted almost a week now. It's a continuous cycle of evening drizzle that settles on the glaze already there, followed by morning sun that melts it just enough to turn it into a treacherous water slide. Ronnie, always a cautious driver, slows to less than a baby's crawl to creep around the end of a wire that's fallen into the street. Ian's told me it's just a ground wire, not live, but it looks dangerous, and I grip the doorhandle tightly.

It's been sixteen years since Ronnie and I met at the Collingwood poetry weekend, a meeting that has led to a long literary friendship and numerous shared poetry events. She's still a vibrant performer, her poetry springing off the page as she reads it. I'm thinking of all this as we creep along the street because we wouldn't be out today, in a car or on foot, except for the reading we're both scheduled to do. The one thing neither of us (hardly) ever does is cancel a reading.

The storm has locked old and frail people into their homes, afraid of falls on the tipped, frozen sidewalks. Our lights still work, perhaps because we're so close to the pole, so Ian's mother is staying with us until her power is on again, and the neighbour behind has stretched a 100-foot cord from our outdoor outlet to his furnace.

The world turned glass around us glistens and drips in the sun like a myth world, a story. Ronnie is concentrating fiercely on her driving. I open the car window to let in the treacherous sun and soft air. The wind is rising. Chimes along the street bell above the low purr of the motor; encased twigs knock against each other with a discernible tinkle. The air, waking like a playful cat, begins to bat the branches together. In my mind, deadly slivers of ice pierce my heart as I imagine the maple in the yard cracking under its burden and crashing through our living room window. The branches above me creak, and now, I think, now it may all indeed come down, trees dead as they stand, trees knives as they stand.

Belmont Avenue runs right beside Windsor Park, which offers an open run for wind off the Rideau River and, behind the houses, a stand of immense cottonwoods to bend to its shove and catch its sound. "Not a single tree on Oor Wullie's street," Ian said last night when the wind started to howl, referring to the bleak pavements of the Scottish mining town captured in a comic strip from his youth in Britain. Nothing to come down on anyone's head. Grey Owl, from my childhood myths, eyes us both smugly from the cover of the Karsh catalogue I edited at the Gallery a decade earlier. The British/Indian poseur looks straight out at the reader with the conviction of the first European environmentalist living his self-chosen lie. I wonder what he'd think of the ice storm that leaves half a million powerless in the cold, and imagine him snug inside a smoky tipi with his bundled wife and child.

Here's Riverdale at last, sanded and salted and a safe path to the National Library where Ronnie has organized a "Poems of Love and Lust" group reading for the League of Canadian Poets. It's taken us ten long minutes to negotiate two blocks, from the ice-covered sand by Bristol Beach where snapping turtles lay their eggs each summer, to this relative highway. Ronnie pulls to a stop with an enormous sigh. As she prepares to turn down Riverdale, I look back at my street with its arctic coat. What moment starts a poem? Through these icy glasses, Ottawa in winter is soldiers dying on the Russian steppes, is dinosaurs caked in sleet sinking down to die, is an American farm boy swinging on a winter-bent birch. Is stories and poems waiting to be written.

Ronnie turns the corner. Still watching the road, I fumble in my bag for the pen I know is in there, the tiny bent notebook. Just big enough for a few scribbled words.

One small black squirrel skitters across the road on flailing claws. *Not another animal stirs*, I write, *not a single bird.*

Riverside Hospital

Sometimes one poem holds a whole life in its hands.

I didn't know we could be so quiet with each other. You never do know, until it you're in it. We lie side by side on the bed, not speaking, not moving, not touching. Not sleeping.

Surely she'll be better. Yesterday morning, we left her reluctantly with Ian's mother, and headed for work. Ian phoned. Morel is worse, he's taking her in, will meet me at the Riverside Hospital.

When I arrive, holding my breath, she's huddled in the waiting room, too crooked to accept my arms. At least they take her right away. She tries to cheer me up, tells me it's okay. My fifteen-year-old daughter, white and absolutely still on the gurney, rousing only to try to comfort me, and then in small gasps. Into a cubicle where she begins to shiver, one thin blanket on the bed. I pull off my coat, pile it with hers on top of her, wrap my scarf around her neck, pull my gloves over her feet. She still shakes, and I fold my body over her, cover as much as I can with my arms. My long-legged girl, curled in like a kitten. Moaning.

At last the doctor. She smiles for him, he presses her stomach, she cries out, he takes blood, disappears. I pile everything back on top of her, wrap myself around as well, trying to stay still, not even breathe hard, so I don't jar her. Ten more long minutes, and a nurse comes in with a needle, and pills. Morel's blood count is up, we need to take care of that right away.

It loops and it loops in my head, why didn't I take her to the hospital earlier, why did I wait? I go over yesterday, over and over.

The long night, on a foam mattress in her room, waking every hour, every two hours. Does it still hurt? No better? Phoning the nurses' line, don't worry, there's an abdominal flu going around. Phoning the doctor, who's out of town, though his locum reassures us. Wondering, is four hours, six hours in Emergency worse or better for her than this endless night?

And now she's being admitted to the hospital, wheeled down the halls and into the elevator. The orderly hits the gurney against the elevator door, and she cries out. We crowd in beside her, I put my hand on her hair. Down the next hall into a double room. The morphine in her veins is making her eyelids droop. A nurse comes in to hook her up to a drip. Ian goes back and forth for coffee, takes my place holding her hand when I go to the bathroom. We pull up chairs on either side of the bed, try not to disturb the snoring shape beyond the other curtain. Sit with her, eyes meeting briefly before we look back at her. Finally the pain begins to ease and she falls asleep. It's 5:30 in the morning. Our doctor still hasn't arrived; later I discover the desk didn't call him and we should have done so. Other doctors come by and tell us to go home, get some sleep. One is the specialist; he's old and gruff, but the nurse says he's the best. He looks at her charts, goes out of the room to ask a question, assures us it's not appendicitis. Maybe an infection, but this antibiotic is new and the strongest they have. Come back in the morning. Get some rest.

I phone my parents, and Ian's mother. They should know, no-one else. Aven is back at university, immersed in assignments; what good would it do to tell her, to have her wait with us, useless, helpless? Let her do her work, and not worry. I can protect Aven, at least.

Ian and I hold hands, when we are not in the hospital room. We still don't speak, except for practical reasons.

I do not say, even to myself, what if she dies.

Certainly, I do not say it to Ian. Do not even acknowledge the words. Cannot let them exist. Armour myself in a rigid shell that keeps me upright and moving.

Three days. She looks like a bruise. Like a spot so tender all over it cannot bear touch. I lay fingers on top of hers, lightly, do not try to enclose her hand in mine. At least she is warm, now; and the morphine helps sometimes.

The specialist comes to see us. She's been moved to a private room; too much pain. Too hard to control. Nothing is improving.

Come out into the hall, he says. I have to do a test on her. I thought it had been done, but now I discover it wasn't done. It will hurt her. I will be as quick as I can. I want you to stay out here.

Hurt her? More?

We wait outside. She shrieks. I bury my head in Ian's chest.

The doctor comes out. It's appendicitis and the appendix has burst. The test wasn't done. He's very sorry. It's critical. They will operate immediately.

I push past him into the room. Rock her, rock her.

Laugh in the face of the devil.
Laugh in the face of death…

It's hour two of the operation, and the waiting room lights are dim. I've found a just working pen, if I shake it, and a newspaper I can write in the margins of. A few lines.

...Sing in the mouth of the monster,
dance in the arms of fear...

Another half hour.

...In the darkness
a space
a quiet space
that globes a quiet flame...

Is that the doctor? I crush the newspaper page, shove it into my pocket. Ian puts his arm around my shoulder.

...in the roaring storm
a word
under the roar of pain...

She was so full of infection we had to open her right up. If wasn't for the new antibiotics, she would have certainly died. But she'll be all right now. You can see her in a couple of hours. He's smiling.

Later, I call her sister. She is furious. Stunned. My Aven, who seldom shows anger, who hasn't shouted at me since she was a raging toddler. How could you keep this from me? Why didn't you tell me? My sister might have died and you didn't tell me! I had a right to be there!

...all I can give
is all I have
child, all I have is yours...

She's right, of course.

> *...in thy hands, O Lord,*
> *I beg thee...*

I tell her so. Tell her I was wrong. Tell her I didn't know what to do.

> *...carry my child*
> *to light.*

Three weeks later, Ian and I are back in the hospital room on, we hope, our last visit with Morel. He's been teasing her, making her giggle. Tomorrow she comes home. *Laugh in the face of the devil*, I tell her, *dance in the arms of fear*, and she laughs at me, we both laugh. It's a brilliant January day. As Ian and I walk to the car, arms locked around each other, bouncing on our toes, leaning into each other like dancers or children, I push away for a moment to fish in my bag for my notebook.

93

> *all is blue*
> *sky sings*
> *and I*

It springs from my pen like a crocus through snow.

Sing the Song of Love

Defining the southeast corner of Confederation Square is the National Arts Centre, where I nearly ruin my daughter's wedding.

I'm panting like a runner, stuck clinging to the stair railing with my mind a total blank and just seconds to go before I'm on at the most important gig of my life: reading the poem I wrote specially at their request for the wedding of Aven and her beloved Mark – and I don't have the poem.

Where is it? Not in the tiny bag I placed decorously on my lap minutes ago when I took my mother-of-the-bride's place in the front row of chairs in the Salon. The high arched lobby of the National Arts Centre, glittering glass sculptures and all, reels in front of my eyes. If the poem is in the car park below, it's a ten-minute run there and back in my useless high heels and long dress. I'll miss the vows, miss reading the poem – how much is the fare to Australia? Think! I have never felt this way before with my eyes open – as if I'm in a terrifying nightmare where I can't catch up to the disappearing figures, can't find my missing test paper, can't remember my lines in the play.

But I can't cling here. If not in the car, where? Where was I just before stepping out of the little dressing room beside the Salon to take my seat of honour at the very front? Before walking across the line of chairs in a stately fashion, nodding here and there, arm resting lightly on Ian's sleeve, head up, smile wide...

The side room. That's where it is!

There's nothing for it but to walk straight back into the Salon through the crack in the huge sculptured doors, and slip as quickly as I can up the side aisle, trying not to click my heels on the stone floors or pant too loudly, straight into the little dressing room – and there it is. One deep breath, then across the front row again as if I know what I'm doing, neck and cheeks flushed up I'm sure into a flaming red.

The minister is still speaking. It must have taken less time than I thought. Or is she spacing her words to cover me?

And now Ian stands to play: "My love is like a red, red rose," blown pure and clean through the silver whistle I gave him for our twenty-fifth anniversary. The tune ripples like water against the arch of the high ceiling, gently brushes and softens as it falls down the huge scarlet and jewel-hued tapestry behind the bride and groom. A brief pause and then I'm on my feet, reading with a greater surge of energy than I've ever given to a poem before.

> *Sing the song of love*
> *Sing the glorious trill of glad love…*

How the bride and groom glow! I smile at them, close the booklet, sit down with Ian's steadying hand under my elbow. Now I can listen to the rest of ceremony they wrote together, and the music, written by my new son-in-law and sung by their friends.

Afterwards, I kiss Aven, gorgeous and flushed in her creamy dress, hug her handsome husband, apologize for the fuss.

"I never noticed anything," she replies.

"No, I didn't either," he says.

Their backs were turned through the whole minute or so of my nightmare, and they are actually unaware that anything went wrong.

"I was just going to keep on playing verses of 'Red Red Rose' until you got back," says my husband, used to being my white knight.

"Mom, are you okay?" Morel, my younger daughter, who never misses anything.

"I knew you'd forgotten something. That's our Susan, I thought." Bridget laughs; as my riding instructor, she knows better than most how I react to stress.

Time to shut up. To everyone but me, the wedding was a beautiful, smooth, and perfectly orchestrated combination of cultures, religions, and personal and communal blessings. In fact, several guests come up to compliment me on my intense, deeply felt delivery of the poem.

The curving stairs are busy now, as the photographer stages romantic tableaus – "now turn and look up at him, that's right, hold the bouquet a bit higher, and gather your skirt with the other. Now you, sir, place one hand on her shoulder and lean forward."

Half a dozen child guests run around the lobby while we wait, under the stairs (never again will I look at them without remembering that moment of hysteria), through the glass doors, into the carpeted bar area and back again.

Just as the kids begin their third whooping round, the photography is finally done, and I tail along behind the crowd that's moving up to the second level for conversation and drinks and hors d'oeuvres before dinner. Soon it will be time for the speeches and toasts… which, thank the heavens above, I neither have to write, nor read.

Continuing Lines

There are four gargoyles on the Peace Tower, a stylized bird,
a stylized human being, a stylized lion, and a stylized dragon.
Each is approximately 8.3 feet long by 2.5 feet high
by 1.5 feet thick. They have been carved from Stanstead grey
granite from Beebe, Québec.

– Explore the Hill: Peace Tower, PWGSC

The Hummingbird Murders

The Hummingbird Murders, *my second poetry collection, had its start before* **Dark Galaxies,** *my first, was out. In 1979, through our neighbours Bob and Deb Bullen, we found a lot on Lac Vert, an almost untouched lake up the Ottawa Valley north of Pembroke on the Quebec side. In 1982, I decided to spend the summer up there. Two and half months with the kids, while Ian, who had courses to teach, commuted from Ottawa.*

I'd spend the summer writing.

All I seem to do is sleep. Morel is two and half, Aven almost six, and most nights I fall into bed like they do as soon as the sun goes down. Having no light but kerosene or candles helps. They get up with the sun too, but I lie dozing in bed for another hour or so, while they root around for muesli and juice and peanut butter sandwiches. Creative neglect, I call it. The story is all. Whatever, I get almost twelve hours of sleep each night.

And more. Often, when the afternoon heat beats through the roof and curls up inside, when the flies on the beach are too vicious to let us swim, we all three flop on the couches or pillows on the cooler floor, for an hour or two longer. Fourteen hours of sleep, day after day.

Sometimes I climb up the swing-down ladder to our bed, to nap and daydream. It's hotter, but private.

One summer I spent
  the whole time in the loft
  with swarms of luscious men...

Private more or less. There are no walls anywhere yet. It's a small, domestic world: the plywood box of the cabin, the path to the outhouse, the path to the sandy strip of beach and jut of Shield rock. Even dozing, I can hear the girls' voices all the time; if they shout or cry, I wake up, if they fall silent, I wake up.

I'm not much good at playing with children – Ian's better – so when he's away, they make their own amusement. Aven collects herbs from the woods around for herb teas, or pretends to be a pioneer and makes plates out of leaves and chairs out of stumps. Morel tags along behind. One thing I've done, though, that interests us all, is to hang a hummingbird feeder outside the big window. And the birds have started to come.

So have the words. Almost a month into the summer, I finally feel rested enough to stay up into the night. Backed by a low fire, I look past my reflection in the window to thick black dark, edged beyond the trees by moon and stars. The absolute quiet is made deeper by the occasional call of a loon or nighthawk.

Ian and I are going through a rough time. "It's one of those dangerous times," I write, and "let's talk about real things." After the first breakthrough evening, I write fast, constantly, on the beach, in the outhouse, no longer waiting for silence and night, no longer carving careful words out of metaphor but simply pouring them onto the page like an unstable sand pile.

I still sleep for ten or twelve hours every night, still crash onto anything soft in the heat of mid-afternoon. But in between I write. Rough and unformed, the poems are beginning to emerge from their cocoons of winter despair, fragile wings tattering in the winds of criticism whenever I look closely. But some are beginning to fly. As I write more, the poems turn darker, do their magic and slip away with my black dreams and thoughts and lock them into words that can be read, re-read, revised. I lift out of my gloom, surprising Ian with my increasing good cheer when he returns from the city each week bringing adult conversation and ice cream. The sheaf of paper thickens. I tremble on the edge of falling back in love with my husband.

But it's not enough. The poems are disorganized, incoherent, unfocussed; they jump from image to image. Anarchists, not a community. I try writing about the birds and animals and scenery that surround me on every side, but can't seem to make it work.

After a while, it begins to seem too much.
The purple flowering raspberries
bloom and bloom,
the lake is unremitting – blue
or slate or white...

The hummingbirds are a crowd now, and we have trouble keeping the feeder filled. This close up, they lose their ethereal perfection. Bird books, I discover, note that hummingbirds are, in fact, greedy, territorial, aggressive. I begin to focus in on the tension between the imagined and real.

Those first few glimpses
the hummingbirds gleamed
iridescent, magic,
beyond our reach.

And then one morning – a dead one, halfway down the path. I see I've become involved, made them stand for something, and now must pay the price – pay attention, pick it up, see clearly at last the green back, speckled neck, white and black banded tail, thorn of beak, tube of tongue, spider curl of feet – and hole behind its head.

And I have my title. My organizing metaphor. The hummingbird murders. The second book is on its way.

Before the summer ended, I wrote the last poem in the book, in which "we lean shoulder to shoulder, look across the lake, which laps at rock, gathers sky, is fed, and flows through a hundred streams." Poetry works for me partly by offering a way to place my confusion beyond myself, untangle it from the background, so I can examine and alleviate it.

Maybe that's what political poems can do, poems that name violence and conflict in crafted, and therefore bearable, words. Bring the truth, in all its complexity, into the light, so we can begin to figure out what to do.

I don't know. I just know that, by the end of the summer, we were a family again.

Gas and Danger in Ottawa South

The Hummingbird Murders went through seven complete edits before it was finally published in 1992 – indeed ten full years after I wrote that first manuscript by hand. Partly I was busy with First Draft and scripts for the GCTC and NAC Atelier and three books for Balmuir Press, and Pass this way again, North/South, and Dark Galaxies, as well as editing jobs and two children.

Partly, the hummingbird poems stalled when I sent them off to several different writing friends, and revised and revised, adding and removing poems and lines and reshuffling the manuscript according to their varied ideas, until I was bamboozled.

And partly, I froze in the middle of the process and found myself unable to write.

An attempt to break that freeze was one reason I entered the Pulp Press Three Day Novel contest in 1984 – which brought me back, by a series of strange coincidences, to Lac Vert. bp had won the first contest, staged the previous year, with an allegorical tale about a love triangle that ended in misery. Mine would be a murder mystery based on the local aerobics class. Write what you know and all that. The contest ran for the whole of Labour Day weekend. I'd stay in Ottawa; Ian would take the kids, then eight and four, to the cottage so I could concentrate.

On Friday at midnight, I started.

The ribbon seems pale. I hope it lasts the weekend. The small oak desk I write at belonged to my friend Gwen Frankton as a child, and her initials are still inked into the top. Her card wishing me luck this weekend is taped to the wall: a bird on a perch in Persian embroidery, a bee among stitchery flowers. Beyond the window, a Manitoba maple drips sap on Ian's new deck – one of many trees filling the vista of back yards in the inner block between here and Hopewell Avenue. Across from me, still lit, I can see the kitchen window of the home of Nancy Ross, my writer friend from the Hopewell Writers Group. Seeing her light gives me a push.

The rough manuscript starts with a midnight entry:

> 12:01 pm Saturday. I mean
> a.m. Oh bed felt good –

I've decided to write this as a double story, in two columns, with the murder mystery on the left and the journal of my writing weekend on the right. De-constructionism, Ottawa-style. My protagonist for the mystery is Ellen, who takes exercise classes at the community centre led by the lovely Louise. So, on the left:

Late again, but it's okay,
they're still on the swinging
warm-up, one foot forward,
one to the side, behind –

And back to the right column, the running journal:

> 1:30 a.m. Damn, where's the
> white-out, I thought I bought
> four bottles –

The murder mystery setting and situation is a direct steal from the dancercise classes I attend at The Firehall on Sunnyside across Bank Street. There's a babysitter for the hour, and three mornings a week, I join poet Ronnie Brown and artist Aili Kurtis and other women from the neighbourhood to bounce and stretch. When *Dark Galaxies* is published by Ouroboros in 1987, they'll hold a post-class tea for me, to celebrate. But right now, I'm busy pinning them all to the page in print. The narrator of the story is an only slightly disguised me:

> But at home, in the half
> gloom of a February living
> room, latched to a being
> who nuzzled and cried and
> hung heavy in your arms,
> but never never talked...

And the writer's voice again:

> 3:39 a.m. I suppose a young
> single person would find
> it easy enough to hack out
> a three-day weekend to write
> a novel in...

By ten-thirty Saturday morning, I've eaten a bag of peanuts and half a basket of peaches and thrown out two half pots of cold tea, slept for a four and half hours, dumped Louise 28 pages into a predicament, and thrust Ellen into sleuth mode –

I was right to worry, Ellen thought. Not only have I been watching the disintegration of an exercise class –

– when reality hits like an explosion.

10:52 a.m. My God. Bob Bullen just called from the Pembroke hospital. I almost didn't answer. I almost took the phone off the hook last night. He doesn't know yet what happened. They're alive. My family. They have blue lips. He's going to call back. Maybe gas. Last night, perhaps, just when I was writing 'what if they're all killed.' My God the baby. The smaller you are the more likely you are to have brain damage, or die. My God. My God.

I have no car, no way to get there. I write the above while I'm waiting to hear again from Bob. He's our neighbour at Lac Vert. His cottage is just up the cliff beside our bay.

11:04 a.m. Called Mom. Coming over. Waiting to hear.

The clack of typewriter keys helps me fight against the urge to scream and cry and start running the ninety miles to the lake on foot. Where's Mom? She only lives ten minutes away by car. Why isn't she here yet?

11:16 a.m. Ian called. Sounds weak, but says they're all right. No-one lost consciousness, just woke with nausea and vomiting. Doctor said it could have been the propane. Ian says Morel's back to normal, Aven almost so, he still feels bad. Wants to stay for the weekend, though. Has promised to turn off the gas, not use the fridge or stove. But I didn't say to get the tank away from the cottage. Maybe it's leaking, could explode. Mom still isn't here. If she doesn't come, maybe I can borrow Andrew's car. Or John and Marie's.
11:25 a.m. Mom's here. We're going up.

We drive to the cottage. Ian has urged me to stay and finish my novel. But I can't do it. I can't go on writing without seeing him and the girls with my own eyes. Mom – Grandma Betty – feels the same.

"I'm here with your family. It seems there was a bit of a propane leak last night. They all got some of it." That's what Bob said, I tell my mother. All of them at once. I couldn't take it in. It was unreal. All of them? Just like that, at once? No. Impossible.

My mother has her own story. As she was driving as fast as she could to my place, she hit a roadblock. Police, with drawn rifles and guns. She doesn't know why, they wouldn't say. That's why it took her so long.

"All the way, I kept thinking, don't take the girls, take me," she tells me.

Out of the blue. As we cross the Ottawa river towards Aylmer, we're stopped two more times by stony-faced policemen with drawn guns. Two years ago, the military attaché at the Turkish Embassy was killed in an armed assault, and there were the same kind of roadblocks. Is it something like that? They won't answer, just say we'll read about it in the newspapers.

It's two-and-a-half hours up the Ottawa River to Fort Coulonge, then Waltham, then north on the Black River Road, to Green Lake. For once, the undulating farms and steep wooded hills that edge Highway 148 as it heads west up the Ottawa Valley rush past without a comment from either of us. The road on the Quebec side of the river runs high and close to the water, and opens onto vista after vista of blue water and white sails – boaters out for the holiday weekend. Straw-coloured stands of corn and acres of lemon-bright rapeseed and fields of horses and cows dozing in the sun and wind pass by unnoticed. As we climb into the Gatineaus, gearing down for two steep climbs, first at Bryson and again at Portage du Fort, the bush closes in. At these higher altitudes, the nights have already dipped below zero, and red maples and sumacs are beginning to flame, while poplars are edging into yellow flags.

Finally, a mile past the Black River Hotel, we turn up the rough track to Bob and Deb's place. There's no road to our lot yet; normally we cross from the landing by canoe, but the canoe will be at the cottage now. Mom and I check with Bob: Ian and the children are back, and recovering in the sun down the hill.

Betty and I make our careful way down the cliff. It's a classic Ottawa Valley lake, a Canadian Shield lake, deep and clear, green, yes, but also brown and blue, clean enough to drink the water. Surrounded by rock shelves and stretches of sand, fed by many streams and two waterfalls, full of trout and pickerel and bass. A few cottages set back among the trees.

Ian and the girls are wrapped in blankets and sitting in beach chairs in the sun. At last I hear the full story. Morel tells me it's the corn they ate last night that made them sick. In fact, Ian's remembered that last week one of our guests moved the fridge, because it looked crooked, and he must have broken a joint in the line that feeds propane from the tank to the house. Last week also, Ian replaced a propane tank that was empty, and in putting it back on, he seems to have broken another joint. The lines are copper, with little give, and the joints simply clamped in place, so a sideways shift can pull one apart. Something we didn't realise. So easy. So easy.

Last night, the propane leaked out and pooled in the cottage. Ian woke up feeling dizzy and nauseous in the middle of the night, and found the kids vomiting and crying and the place full of the smell of gas. He pulled them outside, wrapped them in sleeping bags, then crawled his way up the cliff on his hands and knees, weak as a kitten.

Bob came down the cliff and carried Aven and Morel up again, so he could drive them to the hospital in Pembroke, which he did in the record time of forty-five minutes. Green Lake is surrounded by hills. No phone, no short-wave radio.

"We haven't been gassed," Ian tells me, "not like natural gas. No danger of brain damage. We'll be fine. You should go back to your novel."

Betty has climbed back up the cliff to listen to the radio. She returns to report that someone killed a shopper and wounded two policemen in the Bayshore Mall just before we left town.

It's beyond belief. There I am, immersed in building a fictional world of drama and danger, while around me, two true-life dramas occur, both more theatrical than anything I'm writing, and both involving me. And by bizarre coincidence, the novel I'm writing is structured to allow, in fact require, that I incorporate both these true-life dramas into my fictional one.

Betty ends our argument by offering to stay and take care of Ian and the girls. After a few more protests, I do return to Ottawa in her car, to take up my task again. On the way back I stop at the Restaurant in Fort Coulonge (that's what's on the sign) for coffee and chips, and when the waitress is ringing up my bill, lean over the counter and say, "Do you know what happened to me today? I got a call from Pembroke, from the hospital, my friend said I've got your family here, they've all got some gas, propane, a leak in the line, I was in Ottawa, I've just been up to see them, my husband and two kids…" She's staring at me uneasily, confused. I can see the stripes of blusher on her cheeks, put on carefully and neatly in two solid matching lines. I realize I'm talking very fast, all in a rush, very softly, dropping half my words, slurring others, tumbling them out in a way that makes it almost impossible for her to follow. I've seen drunks do this.

At last she seems to understand I'm talking about my family getting sick from a gas leak. But why am I returning to Ottawa, then? Well my mother is with them now, and I have a project, and –

"Could you give me a Coke to take out?"

She hands me a cold glass bottle with a thick white straw. As I leave, I insist, "It was scary, very scary," and this time she nods and smiles. Maybe at last she understands, or maybe I'm just leaving.

In the car, I strap on my seat belt. Find I don't, after all, have to cry. And drink my deliverance Coke.

I took up my three-day novel again at 9:15 Saturday evening. Looking at the typescript now, I see that the mystery continued as planned, finishing neatly with the arrest of the murderer and reconciliation of the lovers. The right column is full of a disordered mix of guilt ("I still don't know whether I deserve a medal or a whipping for coming back to this project and leaving my family at the cottage"), small details ("Ah, the lovely smell of Ronnie's orange and cinnamon tea"), increasingly woozy philosophizing ("jealousy, succession to a throne, adulterous love – they really don't <u>work</u> in Ottawa South, in 1984"), and worry ("are there enough blankets? – I hope Ian's all right to drive"). The ribbon did run out, and I had to leave the last 13 pages in draft form, with revisions written in by hand. And the title: *Gas and Danger in Ottawa South*.

In life terms, in writing terms, this weekend added another layer of complexity to my decision, made at the death of my cat, that words would never override my connection to those I loved. The finished three-day novel attests to my realization on that Labour Day weekend that, yes, those I love come first, but writing – my chosen labour – comes immediately next. Immediately.

As for the hummingbird murders, my hesitations seemed trivial after this experience. I kept the comments in mind, but returned to my handwritten originals, and started over from scratch. This time, I had a sense of where I was going, and the book moved steadily forward until its publication.

The moment when Bob Hilderley of Quarry Press called to say he wanted the manuscript was one of undiluted delight. His and Susan Hannah's enthusiasm for my poetry through several more books was the foundation on which I built confidence and learned my craft.

Rideau Falls

I have a bad memory for bad things. Without the poems, I wouldn't know what had happened that day. Wouldn't remember the facts. Only my devastation.

25 September 1988. Colin phones me at work; he doesn't want me to hear it on the radio. bpNichol is dead. He died on the operating table. They were trying to fix his back problems, but his heart gave out.

beep – dead. I can't even think. I call Ian, he comes. I leave work and we go to the Rideau Falls, where the noise of the water drowns my noises and the spray hits my face and washes off the salt.

113

> *It comes.*
> *The call.*
> *I climb up the hill*
> *to the Rideau Falls,*
> *it buzzes*
> *from the phone*
> *to my feet*
> *I buzz…*

The next day I take the train to Toronto. I must go to his house, his home, to see Ellie and Sarah. What good it will do I don't know, but I have to go. Colin is with me, Andrew will meet us there. As we pass through Kingston, stopping at the station, I see poet Bronwen Wallace outside the window. She's heard the news, I can tell, and she lifts her arms towards me with an encompassing gesture of comfort and sympathy.

As the train pulls away, I pick up my pen to continue writing down the raw, helpless grief that fills me, somehow shape and control it through a rush of sound and semi nonsense that rattles up from the drive of the train wheels that day –

beep! Dye me right through
with your bumptious words
spindle in through my ears
fill my throat heat and swingle
up through my souls...

In Toronto, I go straight to Ellie, rush into her arms, and we cry and cry. And then on to a theatre where close friends are gathering. The next day, there's a memorial at Harbourfront which requires two large halls, projection into the lobby, and repeated readings to accommodate the thousands who have turned out to mourn.

Within days of returning to Ottawa I receive a quiet poem of sympathy from Betsy Struthers, who lives in Peterborough, and who has become my close poetry friend after we started attending League of Canadian Poets meetings together in the early eighties. In recent years we've been meeting and exchanging our work regularly, so she understands what I've lost. The poem reminds me that finding the right words does comfort.

Later I write other poems at Lac Vert, where I received my first gift of poetry from beep, the small, handsewn chapbook *still*. One piece starts with a quote from his work, "Out of the sleeping body dreams erupt," and continues,

I feel, tonight, your ghost
slip kindly into mine,
shrug me on like a coat,
hands reach into my sleeves,
fingers sheath into mine like gloves...

In the mid-nineties, we do some of these pieces with SugarBeat Music & Poetry as performance poems. Almost songs. I still cry for beep sometimes, but mostly, I feel him as a benign presence, a word to the wise. A well known, well loved, tune. Some friends get under your skin and never truly go.

... for one green beat
I hear your music,
*   with my ears.*

115

Voyageur 2

When Bronwen Wallace semaphored her sympathy to me in the Kingston train station, I didn't know yet, she didn't know, that within ten months, she too, my newest close poetry friend, would be gone.

Bronwen and I had first had a long conversation on that very same train, coming home from a literary jury session in Toronto. Not long after, I visited her in Kingston for a weekend of shared writing and criticism. I'd brought the hummingbird manuscript written at Lac Vert that I was trying to wrestle into coherence. bp had looked at the poems, and offered encouragement but little detail. Did this mean they were terrible and he was simply being kind? When Bronwen told me she really liked the manuscript, and, like beep, had almost no comment but that I was doing something interesting, and wonderful, I burst into tears like a little kid.

*In return, I'd been enthusiastic about the short stories she showed me, the first I'd seen of hers, though I'd loved her poetry for years. I'd used three poems in the Great Canadian Theatre Production **Dangerous Graces** in 1987; ironically, one of them was centred around the gesture language of the gorilla Koko, recalling later for me the gestures she used to communicate her sympathy to me through the train window.*

Bronwen tells me she's dying. It's the spring of 1989, and I've called to see if we can get together to talk poetry. She doesn't really want to see people, however; a vicious melanomic cancer is attacking her face. Her friend and mine, the poet Carolyn Smart, is arranging Bronwen's care with a bevy of friends in Kingston. I talk to Carolyn a few times, and keep in touch with Bronwen by phone and an occasional note, including a poem about our meeting on a train.

We have a good conversation not long before she dies. I've just come back from the League of Canadian Poets annual meeting, and she wants to know everything about it, specifically, the gossip. When I run out, she tells me one of her short stories from the set I'd seen is shortlisted for the Journey Prize, and she hopes to win in order to leave the prize money for her son.

Shortly after, in the warmth of an August night, I join a group of Ottawa poets at Blaine's house to share poetry. We gather in his garden off Byron Avenue, which is filled with blossoms and scent, and read to the light of candles. We talk of Bronwen. As we read, and talk, it grows darker. We're outside partly because tonight there's an eclipse of the moon.

And still I keep hoping
still can't quite believe
you will actually go,
even as we sit
together in the garden
one night while you lie drifting,
sit talking of you,
watching the moon
subsume in earth's shadow,
round out, glow.

During that same week, the third week of August 1989, the space probe Voyageur 2 is passing around Neptune and Triton before heading off into deep space, to be gone beyond the reach of our instruments forever. The last images are coming in to the media, strange, unlike anything we've seen before.

For a few days more
you send us visions
from the very edge –

These blend in my mind, all these elements, the eclipse of an
explorer, a poet who writes like no-one else, a light in our sky moving
on into a darkness that's total to us but maybe not to her.

On 25 August, Carolyn phones. It's a warm, lovely day, sun, soft
wind.

then, this morning,
you step off the last orbit
that might have brought you back,
curve away alone
into the gleaming dark –

I drive out to Westar, where I'm leasing a horse named Chico,
take him for a ride around a field far from the barn. Around, around
again, trusting his eyes because I can't see too well. And no-one can
hear me here, except him.

I have to believe
as you plunge behind the stars.

Bronwen's memorial in Kingston was held in a theatre, and
attended by more than 700 people. Ten months after bp. She didn't
win the Journey Prize, but Margaret Atwood wrote a tribute that
began by saying Canada had lost a wonderful poet today. I heard
she'd shown it to Bronwen before she died.

Then, I went back to struggling with my hummingbird manuscript. It was missing something. I took it back to Lac Vert with me, where the series had begun. Late one night, to the light of kerosene lamps, I wrote out the night-time laments that now interleave the more narrative sequences in the finished book. The grief was for Bronwen, gone before I really even knew her, but somehow they added the dimension of threatened grief to my tale of a marriage in trouble, an image of what would be lost were it to fail. Bronwen's own poems weave many voices and elements together. I hope she wouldn't mind me co-opting the poems I wrote for her into the manuscript she'd encouraged me to believe was good. When *The Hummingbird Murders* was finally published by Quarry Press, in 1992, I dedicated it to both Bronwen and bp.

Like him, she was just 44 when she died. Her work had already passed into the canon; what else would she have written, given time?

Learning to Ride

My relationship with horses began before I remember. The milkman delivered, and he did it in a horse-drawn cart. I always went out to greet the horse, even though it wasn't a beautiful horse, or a friendly horse, or an accessible one – it was doing a job and uninterested in the scruffy kids on the curb. It wore blinkers, and like its owner, was grumpy and bony and graying. Both might snap or nip, with words, or teeth. But – a horse! It left mild, musky piles in the road, quickly scooped up by our immigrant neighbours. For the garden, my mother told me. They had no gardens that I could see, though I wonder now if there were pots or barrels of tomatoes or potatoes. Then I just accepted her explanation as a mystery.

One day I'm telling Blaine about how much I love riding. Why don't you write about it? he asks. I imagine poems with titles like "Ode to My Horse" and "A Sweet Pony for Girls." I can't do that, I tell him. The literary community will laugh at me. The only contemporary serious "horse" poems I've read use the animals as dream figures or symbols, rather than the down-to-earth, food-centred, smelly and muddy beasts I know. It seems like a completely separate part of my life, I say. For example, the first time Gwen came to see me ride, she was shocked by the language my instructor used: "He was shouting at you," she told me, "He never even said please or thank you. It was awful." I explain to Blaine that I was amazed, because I felt I'd had a fantastic lesson and that Jeff had been unusually complimentary. How could she hear what he said so differently?

So the interesting thing, Blaine replies, is that the language you use in the stable is different than the language you use with your friend and me, and maybe with other literary and arts friends. Yes, I say, it's more direct and clear; functional, no sidelights or parenthetical comments. Just straight to the point.

So why not write about that, he asks?

That afternoon, I begin a new poem:

Learn a new language
the language of the body
the speech of the muscles…

Around the same time, my mother renews an old connection, with Robert and Marion Verrall. Both artists, they had been close friends of my parents before they moved to Montreal, where Bob had worked for the National Film Board. Now he's retired, and they've bought a country home in the eastern townships. Near them is a stable, and Bob has ridden his first horse at the age of 67, and fallen in love with riding. When he hears that I'm writing a set of horse poems, he invites us to visit. Later Bob and Marion visit Westar. Before long, we're exchanging what eventually becomes 26 poems and 26 black and white drawings. *Learning to Ride* comes out from Quarry Press in 1994. It's designed by Paul Verrall and dedicated to Jeff and Bridget McKessock and Westar Farms, with special thanks to riding friends Carol, Nancy, Jan, Shirley, Peggy, and Robin, many of whom come out to watch me launch the book at the National Library, riding crop in hand.

I read from the book on a trip across Canada that summer. To my surprise, it's well reviewed not only in magazines like *Horse & Country* and *Horse Sport* but in newspapers like the *Ottawa Citizen* and literary publications like *Books in Canada* and the Canadian Library Association publication. "Learn a new language" is chosen for the 1994 *Windhorse* anthology and "Dismounting" for the *Toronto Star* poetry corner. Blaine was correct: no area of life or human experience is beyond the reach of poetry – if the approach is right.

As far as I know, Westar holds the only horse show that offers a poetry book as one of the prizes every year. Because I'm a better writer than rider, and sometimes confuse the two ("How's your riding going?" "Oh fine, I have a book coming out next year." "How's writing these days?" "Excellent, I jumped a three-foot oxer on Wednesday"), the prize celebrates not the first place winner, but someone who makes it around the course with only one or two missteps, usually a fourth place novice. "The Sum Shy 'Nearly Perfect' Prize" has been going for almost a decade now.

SugarBeat and Geode Music & Poetry

Of all the chapters in the book, this was hardest to write. It was difficult because I'm still involved with Geode, which is an extension of SugarBeat, so it's hard to find any perspective. What are we doing, and is it anything more than enjoying the age-old partnership between music and words; are we Neanderthal songwriters, in fact?

And whether we are or not, which among the many stories and activities of the last decade would best represent the whole?

Without answers, I have simply leapt in, as a famous queen once suggested, at the beginning.

I first hear SugarBeat Music & Poetry perform at the Ottawa Jazz Festival in 1995. Poet Colin Morton reads from his poems based blues and jazz, and Gavin McLintock on saxophone, Jennifer Giles on keyboard, and Alrick Huebener on bass lay down grooves behind him. The mix is evocative, intriguing in the soft summer dusk. First Draft more or less folded five years ago, and I miss seeing Colin and Alrick regularly, I miss working with other creative people. Much as I make plans to see my friends in purely social contexts ("We must get together for lunch!"), the truth is, I work all the time, if poetry is work, so most of my socializing occurs in collaborative projects.

Mind you, the break has been good for me. Undistracted, I've published two poetry collections, I've begun working full-time at the Gallery and started some art-poetry projects there, I'm editing a chapbook series with the League of Canadian Poets, I've even had some time to spend with my teenage girls and husband.

SugarBeat does a few more gigs – at the Great Canadian Theatre Company, for example – and then Colin leaves for a year to be a writer-in-residence in the States.

Within a month or so, Alrick calls to say they'd like to continue with me, if I'm interested. Jennifer teaches music and composition at Carleton, and turns out to be one of the most creative and flexible people I know. She also has that charismatic glow that the best teachers carry around like a cloud of scent.

Gavin has his own engaging charm. He's a rational computer man during the day and a sensitive creative soul on Saturday mornings, eager to head off into the blue skies of experiment and improvisation.

Alrick and I have been working together for so long that we know we can take any risky leap and the other will cushion our fall.

The working method we develop is quite different from the careful notation and scripting of First Draft. No books will come out of this group. It's the contrast between the classical model, where everything is written down as far possible – Andrew's approach – and the jazz model, where basic forms and a shared repertoire comprise the jumping off point for individual expression and unique performances. bpNichol would have liked SugarBeat.

What we do in our weekly sessions is, we turn on the tape recorder. I read a poem. Then I hand out copies and read it again. This time, the others begin to react musically, to the images, sounds, ideas, emotions, even the shapes of the words on the page. We roll back the tape, listen, talk. Maybe a chord sequence suggests itself, maybe a repeated riff. We make a few notes on the margins of the poem, and repeat the process. And again. Week after week, until the settings become predictable enough to take to the stage, while still variable enough to stay interesting.

In these sessions, we're looking not for a backdrop to the poem, but for another voice, a counterpoint, that will stretch and deepen the words, maybe take them somewhere unexpected. Thus, Jennifer's driving 7/4 rhythm under my sleepy poem "The pleasure of lusting after you," brings out an urgent subtext I hadn't known was there. Alrick balances my poem for bp, the one that starts "beep – dye me right through / with your bumptious words," on a comical Klezmer base that's ridiculous and exactly right. Gavin's lyrical melodic line behind my poem "How God Sees" makes the Ottawa Valley seem to open out before my eyes like a flower, even before I speak.

We lost probably seventy per cent of the audio material of First Draft because of taping costs and old technology, so I'm intense about recording as we go. The result to date is three CDs and an audiotape, capturing a repertoire of some seventy pieces developed over ten years and fifty or sixty performances in music clubs, libraries, cafés, bars, galleries, theatres, festivals (the Ottawa Folk Festival and Blue Skies, especially), and on local and national broadcast media.

The joy of collaboration is working with artistic, intense people; the pain of collaboration is working with artistic, intense people. After a few years, SugarBeat takes a tumble and comes up as Geode Music & Poetry. Gavin finds other groups and interests, notably the Jazz Jam, Ottawa Jazz Happenings, and Jazzworks. Jennifer stays a while longer, but then turns her explorations towards music again and is now active in some wild improv bands with Linsey Wellman, Mike Essoudry, and Rory Magill.

With Alrick and me at its core, Geode has kept the same working approach, but instead of meeting weekly, we invite interested and experimental musicians to join us for specific gigs and recording projects. Thus, the first Geode CD includes Mike Essoudry and Petr Cancura, and the second brings in David Broscoe, Jamie Gullikson, Mark Molnar, Jennifer Giles, and John Higney.

Geode has lasted well because it keeps changing. What's inside that dull grey rock, you may wonder. Amethyst, quartz, emerald...? But it may soon be rolling, mossless, on into other hands, or possibly the sunset. Projects last, in my experience, seven to ten years, and I began working with SugarBeat in 1996. Hmmm.

Uncommon Prayer and Mother Tongue Books

Uncommon Prayer, published in 1997 by Quarry Press, is the most disorganized of my books. It came together as a result of dropping all the unpublished poems from the previous decade into a pot, and bringing the pot to a boil. At first glance, there's no common theme – except the secret lives and wishes of chairs. I wanted to call the book "How Chairs Pray," but Bob Hilderley, the Quarry publisher, found that obscure. The second theme was my conviction that poetry – and love and prayer and truth – all consist of paying attention. We compromised on Uncommon Prayer, reflecting both themes with a chair painting by Pat Durr on the cover, and a predatory dandelion from the poem "How Dandelions Prey" by Juliana McDonald on the back. Was it coincidence that my mother had been doing paintings of chairs for years? And that a wall of her red chairs, entitled "Family," had been part of a recent art show at City Hall? (SugarBeat performed a series of chair poems at the opening.)

Looking for a place to launch the book, I immediately thought of Mother Tongue Books / Femmes de paroles.

I stop staring into space and move a small stack of pottery figurines and a basket of bracelets to the back of an armrest so my friends Irene Lillico and Jean Gubby can slide in plates of homemade cookies and savouries. Laura and Evelyn and Julie – the owners of the bookstore – have cleared as many surfaces as they can, but the space is still crammed with books, jewellery, candles, cards. How are we going to squeeze in 38 drawings, 16 paintings, and a pile of artist's books, and leave a corner where I can read?

Many of the artworks on display have a poetry angle. Pat Durr has brought paintings based on haiku, three of Julie McDonald's paintings come from poems of mine, and Roberta Huebener, longtime collaborator, has brought a triptych incorporating one of my haiku, a related painting, and an artist's book on a poem I wrote for her fiftieth birthday. The rest of the drawings and paintings, many of chairs, are by my mother, Betty Page.

It's not yet 2 p.m., but people are already streaming in.

This is one of my favourite places for poetry-and-art events, a long narrow glass-fronted space of warm colours and brown wood that's been warming up a rather dull strip of Bank Street for a few years now. The successor to the revolutionary Ottawa Women's Bookstore that opened on Elgin Street in the eighties, Mother Tongue is the only feminist, bilingual, bookstore in town. I held a reading series here in the early nineties: six poets, with eight minutes each, timed with a real handbell and with a metaphoric hook in reserve if needed. Poet Stephanie Bolster took over for a while and renamed it the Athena Series. She left to teach creative writing at Concordia University, but local and visiting writers still read and launch their books here regularly.

"Okay, we're officially open, come on in!"

People are cramming into the store, spilling out onto the street. There must be fifty or sixty at least. I catch snatches of comments from all sides as I struggle to keep out of the way of those trying to look at the art.

"I drew that chair on the last day of a course I took from Molly Bobak in New Brunswick. I didn't want to leave, but I had a chance to go sailing, which I'd never done before. So I wasn't abandoning the chair. Others would come to sit in it. I had just gone sailing!" Betty, talking with a potential buyer.

Juliana: "I was interested by Susan's 'how chairs pray' series, so I began my own series of praying flowers in the spring ..."

Pat is off on an art retreat (what kind of excuse is that?), so I point viewers to her text in the small catalogue I put together: "Being a frog-lover from way back, the moment I saw the small book of Japanese poetry *One Hundred Frogs*, I was fascinated. This book inspired 22 works."

And me, not from the catalogue: "Let me through please, I need to get to that table, thanks, it's time for the reading...I'd like to welcome you all to 'How Chairs Pray'..."

> *The need of objects to be used,*
> *their longing to embrace*
> *our momentary soft shadows*
> *in plastic and metal arms...*

"I've always thought an old woman's chair would have a very distinct voice – "

> *It's the holding on to*
> *I envy, the springing back*
> *so softly from every press...*

"And what about refinishing – "

> *Nicks, scratches, torn leather, frayed seams –*
> *the faults of years are clear to see...*

"And finally, the skeleton chairs – "

... in black and bony poise
against the yellow birch,
lighthearted chairs,
useless and free.

Four hours later, Betty lifts her beer and we clink glasses.

"Wow! That was a success." The Barley Mow, across the street, has the same mellow, dark wood interior as the bookstore. As always after a good reading, I'm exhilarated. Talkative, downright noisy. I need that beer.

"Mom, you sold 29 of 42 pieces. Twenty-nine. That's phenomenal!"

"And you sold a pile of books!"

Ian and a few others who have joined us for the post-event drink listen in amusement as we congratulate ourselves, the bookstore, the audience and buyers, the bar, the artists, the publishers, the whole universe.

Sudden weariness sends me groping for my coat. A few last "Congratulations" echo behind as we drive away. Ian and I carry the boxes and bags of supplies and few unsold drawings into my mother's place. I kiss her on the cheek – "What a great show! I've never heard of selling 29 pieces in one afternoon" – and start to shut the door.

"But Susan," I hear behind me, "what was wrong with the rest? The ones that didn't sell?"

Ottawa Together

Any snapshot of a literary scene is risky. Colin Morton's 1989 anthology **Capital Poets,** *with works by John Newlove and Chris Levenson, among others, inspired angry letters to the* **Ottawa Citizen,** *because not every published poet in town was included. As Ian says to me when my envy is showing: So why* **are** *you writing poetry, then?*

In the sixties, I knew one published poet in Ottawa – George Johnston. He was my father's generation. Elizabeth Harvor, also a Quaker, was still a secret scribbler. The poetry outlets I knew were *The Charlatan*, to which I submitted one piece (rejected: is there a grudge here?), and Oberon, which seemed way beyond me. Poetry readings were held in the universities, if at all.

When I returned from the west in 1975, things were changing. Chris Levenson had co-founded *Arc Magazine* around then, and started the Arc reading series in 1981, presenting poets from out of town alongside locals like Enid Rutland. Other reading series, many founded by Jane Jordan, such as Tree, Sasquatch, and Orion, also began to bring in readers, supported by the Canada Council, and a literary scene began to grow. It was nurtured as well through Seymour Mayne at Ottawa University, but I didn't know that group at the time. My particular circle of friends, met mainly at the Ottawa Poetry Group and Tree, included a set of poets who were just beginning to publish first books in the eighties: Blaine Marchand, Sandra Nicholls, Nadine McInnis, Ronnie R. Brown, Colin Morton, Margaret Dyment (now Slavin), and John Barton.

Most of us joined the League of Canadian Poets in the eighties as well, where we became known as That Gang From Ottawa; Blaine had t-shirts made for us with that slogan. He later became League president, as did Betsy Struthers, who had left Ottawa for Peterborough but remained attached to our circle. Patrick White was publishing *Anthos* magazine then; I still have posters he did of a poem of mine. John Newlove was around but seldom came to literary events, though we talked when he did some freelance work for *Vernissage*, the Gallery magazine. I came to know Stephen Brockwell by editing his manuscript for Balmuir, and Diana Brebner after her impressive first reading at the League. Marianne Bluger was entering the same Ottawa Valley Writers contests I was, and usually winning. She, like several of the group, also won the Archibald Lampman Award, established for the best Ottawa poetry collection. Around the same time, Blaine co-founded Ottawa Independent Writers, and the Ottawa Book Festival.

The nineties saw many new reading series like the Dusty Owl events, Gallery 101 readings, Janet Irwin's "Poetry in the Park" series (I bought a pair of gold sandals for that show), and National Poetry Month jams at places like the Bayou and Arthur McGregor's Ottawa Folklore Centre. Carleton started a new poets series. The Ottawa Folk Festival gave Geode chances to trade poems with Jane Siberry, and "words in bloom" with gardening expert Ed Lawrence, and to open for the rock star Gowan in the National Library and Archives auditorium. This was one of the wide range of events Randall Ware began to host there: two SugarBeat shows for the League, innumerable book launches, exhibitions from the collections, Ottawa Independent Writers events, and lavish evenings for the Ottawa Book Awards and Governor General's Award presentations.

Recently the Archives has also been one of the central hosts (along with the National Arts Centre) for the Ottawa International Writers' Festival founded and run by Neil and Sean Wilson, Kira Harris, and Thea Yateman. The Writers' Fest has transformed Ottawa into a centre for world literature, while still featuring such local events as the *Convergence* reading and launch of *Waging Peace*, as well as – these were really fun! – two manic on-stage Poetry Jams with George Elliot Clarke and Stuart Ross among others plus the Geode musicians and guitarist Roddy Ellias. Other institutions open to poets include the National Gallery, which has featured poetry in its magazine, its audioguides, and live in its halls (okay, so I had something to do with these), both universities, and the Museum of Civilization.

Starting in the later nineties, younger poets like Stephanie Bolster, Anita Lahey, Shane Rhodes, Craig Poile, and Max Middle began generating their own events, publishing projects, and readings. Max's work will be on the next Geode CD, along with pieces by Penn Kemp and Linsey Wellman. Oni the Haitian Sensation is an exultant spoken-word poet who helps organize the Canadian Slam Poetry WordOlympics; John Akpata and Anthony Bansfield are other drivers of this thriving performance scene.

Poetry activities continue to expand in the 2000s. rob mclennan organizes hundreds of events each year, publishes himself and many other writers on-line and through Chaudière Books, acts as the central internet information source for Ottawa, and runs the Small Books Fair.

Rhonda Douglas is polishing up Tree, which has been held in the basement of the Laurier Royal Oak for years. The Ottawa Art

Gallery hosts the Factory Reading series, the School of Dance has a poet-in-residence program, I've enjoyed doing African music and poetry sessions with Segun Akinlolu and friends, John Armstrong is again setting my poems for choir. The Cube Gallery is the latest poetry-art venue in a long series starting with Le Hibou.

Ottawa has lost several poets recently: Enid Rutland, Marty Flomen, Diana Brebner, John Newlove, and last year Juan O'Neill and Marianne Bluger. Steven Artelle of the Ottawa Literary Heritage Society is working with the Ottawa City Archives to build up a literary archive before we all disappear. Others, like Monty Reid, have arrived.

The media here are largely poetry positive, especially Chez and its Sparks 2 series in the eighties and Jane Crosier at CKCU and Mitchell Caplan at CHUO now. Burt Heward had a long-running books column in the *Citizen*, and now James McGowan and Charles Gordon cover much of what's interesting and literary, as does *The Ottawa Express*. As for the CBC, for decades, I and many others would take the brass elevators to the seventh floor of the Château to read a poem or talk about a project with Ken Rockburn, John LaCharity, or Brent Banbury. Adrian Harewood, now warming up the streetscape of the Sparks Street Mall, has also let a few poets slip inside.

This is a skim view off the top, distant and cloudy, through my own lenses. Apologies for distortions, errors, lacunae. I was going to write that Ottawa is clearly good to poets, from what I can see, but really can't end this chapter with a neat cap-off, because it just keeps going on.

Convergence: Poems for Peace

I was a poet who lived in Ottawa, and the millennium was coming up. I wanted to mark it in some way, with a peacemaking project. During the Persian Gulf war ten years ago I'd written postcards to all the MPs, but anyone anywhere in Canada could that. What could I do, here in the capital city, that other poets couldn't? Well, I could walk up Parliament Hill with poems about peace in my pocket and deliver them directly into the hands and ears of the politicians who work there. And I could do that for other poets, too.

This vague wish for a bit of useful exercise led to a project that took three years out of my life and just about killed me – and my mother. Without her, I would never have been able to do it. **Convergence** *– my co-worker Alan Todd from the Gallery suggested the name – ended up involving hundreds of artists and writers and supporters across the country. Betty and I cut and folded some 3500 individual art-wrapped peace poems, plus 50 complete boxed sets, to fund the project; her thumbs, which pressed all those creases and cut all those corners, have never quite recovered. She alone made about 2500 art prints as wraps; the rest came from artists across Canada. And I printed out so many poems on fancy paper that I wore out two printers. Machines, that is.*

As for the contribution side, my friends in Ottawa came through right away, and the contacts I'd made through the League of Canadian Poets and Quakers and my artist friends meant I had many great poems to choose from, as well as many original artworks. We also had immediate buyers for the sets. The problem was keeping up.

At first, though, it looked like the whole thing would fizzle. This is the note I sent out to supporters after the first apparently disastrous day.

In the end, there'd be a dozen reports like this (though none as glum), and eventually a book.

The sun pours into the Hall of Honour for the first time in days, and a Constable wanders over, bemused. Who are these slightly scruffy people, with their coats in a heap on one chair and a rainbow of art arrayed across two other seats like offerings at a spring flower market?

Convergence: Poems for Peace has arrived today, Thursday, the first of February 2001, on Parliament Hill in the inkjet-stained hands of me, the Ottawa poet and organizer, and Colin Morton, a poet, novelist, and vice-president of the League of Canadian Poets (which is also publishing the project).

Yes, but what is it? Fifty-two poets from across Canada, from Gabriola Island to Charlottetown, are converging with artists from Nunavut to Nanaimo to St. Michael's in Newfoundland, to publish a new poem on the subject of peace each week of 2001, as a gift for Members of Parliament and Senators. Each poem, printed on silk or hemp or wildflower paper, is wrapped in an original art print.

"Please, take a look." I pick up a green, violet, and rose rice-paper poemwrap by Betty Page and open the flaps to Sarah Klassen's poem "Waging Peace."

...You might as well
wage peace as war...

I read it to him out loud. The sun reflects off the polished marble floor up through the paper, warming the colours and picking out the silk fibres. "We're going to hand out a different poem each week while Parliament is sitting, until everyone here has one of their own. A present, maybe a moment to pause and think about what they can do to make a more peaceful world." The words sound hopeful, and thin, under the tall dome. The Constable raises his eyebrows. "Sounds like a plan," he says.

And this is week number one. Eight parliamentarians have agreed to come and find "the woman in the white coat" – me, wearing a cotton lab jacket from a Norwegian resister, embellished by Prince Albert poet Joanna Weston with peaceful words like *shalom* and *paix* and worn by her during twenty years of activism. Now she's passed it on to *Convergence*, and we're asking participants to add their signatures to the mix.

We look up as Nicole Hussey, assistant to the Liberal MP from Nipissing, Bob Wood, strides into the hall, her high heels echoing. She says Bob is in the House, but will be interested in our gift. She chooses a blue-wrapped poem, listens while I read it, tucks it back into its handmade envelope to take to her boss, and wishes us well.

The hour goes by. We rearrange our poems, spread them out on the seats that ring the hall. A few people glance at us curiously, as they pass, but no-one stops. I look up at the bevelled windows and the carved wooden plaques for every province and think of Yeats's line, "for peace comes dropping slow."

There are many worse places to spend an hour waiting than the sunlit heart of Canada. I could be in a line outside a prison for writers who pen the "wrong" words; I could be on my knees under a burning Indian sun trying to lift a slab of concrete with a rusty lever.

I look around the dome. The Hall opens directly from the front door under the Peace Tower, and when I was a child you could walk right in. Today, we had to go through an elaborate security check-in at a side-door basement entrance. It felt shabby somehow. But they did let us in. The Parliamentary Library is just down the corridor; I wonder if the guards would let me visit, supposing no-one else comes. That would make the trip worth it anyway.

"MPs are busy people," says Colin, as the hour, and then the hour and a quarter strike. We pack up our poems. I can't wait any longer, I must go back to work.

"If the bell rings for a vote, they have to go."

"Yes, well, maybe next week."

The Constable raises his hand to us as we leave the Hall. I smile ruefully and he makes a victory sign. At least he heard a bit of poetry. And one person from one MP has listened too, and taken our gift. Maybe, next week, a few more people will join us. Maybe we'll change our approach, find another way to reach the Parliamentarians. Maybe I'll write a poem.

Adagio and *Waging Peace*

I did write a poem, but not the one I expected to write.

Since that somewhat bumpy beginning, **Convergence** *had been moving steadily forward, with increasing success as it became better known. Now, in September, I was looking forward to actually being able to complete handing out peace poems to everyone on the Hill by the end of the millennial year. Ian, too, had been having interesting experiences on the Hill, participating as a bit player in taping episodes of the Pierre Trudeau television miniseries being staged inside and outside the Parliament Buildings.*

Today, I'm thinking about nothing but finishing up my tasks at the Gallery quickly so I can leave and take my daughter Morel to the bus station to return to Montreal, where she now lives. Serge has come into my office with a disturbing but confusing tale about planes crashing, but I don't have time to listen. I tell him I'll listen to the news on the car radio.

Barely noon. There should be time. I pick up Morel in the cafeteria, and we rush out the door and into my car. The traffic on Mackenzie is oddly heavy and slow. The familiar intersection at Rideau is blocked by Mounties and city police, and they're stopping each car before waving it through onto Colonel By. Wellington is cordoned off. Some tourist groups are still walking through the barriers, however, chatting to their guides. It strikes me afterwards that this is somehow Canadian, this refusal to be really ruffled, this assumption of civility and good will.

I turn on the radio. "This morning in New York ..."

The new American Embassy is on our left, Parliament Hill,

where Ian is taping an episode, is on my right, the National Gallery is behind, Morel is in the car... One helicopter would do it.

We make the bus, my daughter and I. My husband has been locked into a room in the West Block all day, his taping cancelled. The cast has watched television for six hours by the time Security allows them to go home. He's seen the planes crash and the towers fall over and over again.

11 September 2001. Not an ordinary day, at all.

A couple of days later I write a poem at the request of artist Roberta Huebener, who was born in New York not far from the twin towers and lived there with her first husband until they came to Canada to escape the Vietnam war. She incorporates the poem into a painting, which sells almost before the paint is dry, so she does a second, different version. The poem and paintings are entitled "Adagio."

> *slow waves drop sleep into the arms of the dead*
> *gulls whirl and cry,* love   love
> *stone is the end of it, fallen stone*
> *fold thy souls into the sea*

Months before, I had arranged a reading of the complete series of poems from *Convergence: Poems for Peace* by as many writers and artists as could attend. It's to be held at the National Arts Centre Fourth Stage, my second time there. The reading is scheduled for 15 September 2001. We decide to go ahead.

It is an extraordinary evening.

The theatre is full. Twenty-six readers come up to the microphone

one after another, in silence, say their name and connection to *Convergence*, and read one or more poems. There is no applause. We go straight through all the poems; it takes about an hour. In that darkened space, with a single spotlight on the low stage, and no words but that of poetry that was all written long before 11 September, a sense of shared, reverent mourning develops. Almost a sense of prayer. It is a powerful experience of how poetry can be the right, and sometimes the only possible, communal language of response to terrible events.

A second reading of the whole series of poems was held in December in Toronto at the Art Bar, and recorded on a CD available through the League of Canadian Poets. The story of *Convergence* is told more fully in the book *Waging Peace: Poetry and Political Action*, a book which would never have come out except fo the urging and immense help of Kingston poet, and later League president, M.E. Csamer. *Waging Peace* was published by Penumbra in 2002. It travelled across the country for a year with Quaker writer Margaret Slavin, who gave it to Meetings along the way; it's been taken to many different countries and places by poet Penn Kemp; it's being used as a university text by Sandra Stephenson in Montreal; and it continues to sell steadily. All royalties have been donated to peace education by the contributors – an array from Margaret Atwood to Liz Zetlin, Jocelyn Aird-Bélanger to Paula Zoubek, Roger Nash to Heather Spears to Senator Grafstein. I'm glad. And I'm glad the task, which started so innocently and grew so large, is done. It's only six years after the millennium.

National Art Centre Fourth Stage

Offbeat poetry events used to be held in the NAC Lobby. I've performed wordmusic there with Andrew McClure and First Draft in the CBC noontime concert series run by Jill Laforty, and helped raise money for a free-speech benefit with SugarBeat bass player Alrick Huebener there also. Now such events tend to be held in the Fourth Stage, which was renovated about ten years ago from the old Elgin Room (itself a renovation of the former bookstore). I've appeared on the Fourth Stage with Talking Marigolds, a group of feisty poetry women (the **Ottawa Express** *took a bared-breast photo for the article, of me and Ronnie among others), with* **Convergence** *in 2001, with Geode in 2004, and – an especially enjoyable event – with CBC Ottawa's 2002 "first ever cross-Canada Poetry Face-Off," with the theme "Love in Ottawa."*

142

Hundreds of people crowd the line-up at the door to the National Art Centre's Fourth Stage. It only holds 150. As one of the participating poets, they have to let me through, but what will happen with Ian and Morel and our friend Dan Page, who have come along to cheer me on – and vote? It's a "crowd choice" contest: the poem that gets the most votes from the audience wins this round, and the poet goes on to compete in a cross-country Face-Off.

CBC Radio usually pulls in good crowds, but no-one – not the organizers, not the poets – expected this kind of response. Ian gets in by pushing to the front and pointing out that he's my husband, but Dan and Morel don't make it, and clearly most of those waiting at the door will also be turned away, possibly as many as a two hundred.

When did poetry become so popular?

Alan Neale, of CBC "Trends" fame at the time (now he's host of Fuse), is wearing a spiffy gangster suit in which I take personal pride, since I advised him to choose it over a couple of other possibilities when I was in the CBC studios at the Château Laurier earlier for a Face-off interview. Alan starts with his usual quick and witty patter, making a game of a golden paper crown which will descend on the chosen one at evening's end. Rats. Morel would have enjoyed this: she was more interested in seeing Alan than me.

First up is Anthony Bansfield (a.k.a. Nth Digri), a powerful performer with a fine ear for lyric and clear, pungent delivery.

Then Kris Northey, with an ethereal, moving reflection on lost love, that paints the corners with ghostly flowers. I notice the crafting in her poem.

We've drawn from a hat for order, and I'm third, not as hard as first and not as discouraging as last.

"And now, a warm welcome please for Susan McMaster!"

"Ah, sex!" I exclaim, "Roundy and humpbacked, sweaty and slick..."

They're not sure whether to laugh or gasp. Surely this goes too far, for Ottawa, for the CBC.

It's a 5-minute slot, I had two weeks to write this poem, and I've decided to just have fun. In the words of one line of the poem, "to skip to the carillons of a capital town." A town full of mildly aging civil servants, professors and teachers and students sporting clean tattered jeans and whimsical tattoos, with a handful of genteel business types thrown in. People like me.

...finnagling sweet talker
keeps swinging me back
to your Apaloosa arms,
your snub-nosed burrower,
your musk-furry croon.

I can see a number of these sympathetic, intelligent, unpressured, Ottawa faces beyond the beams of stage light, each lit from below by the orange tea candles that glow on the little round tables. I search out their excellent haircuts and scarves among the bobbing, gently mohawked youth, and aim my words at them.

Ah, sex, ah love.
We're bouncing and eagled,
flying prone-high –

They're leaning back into their chairs, even the younger crew are grinning.

Ah, lovely, shared, sigh.

After the over-the-top beginning, I send the couple in my poem "to stroll, arm-in-arm (feeling just artsy enough, in an Ottawa kind of way)," down the Canal, "lamp-pooled, willow-leafed," then on to "cruise the Market *rues* under a double-faced moon, two lazy lovers safely *soignés.*"

Ottawa's been called a playground for adults, and looking around this elegant little theatre full of the comfortable and cultured, the phrase rises on its tail and dances. The perfection of the blend between crowd, place, and poem puts an extra *oomph* into my delivery, which isn't surprising, because after all –

> *The NAC has a knack for*
> *pleasing maple-bushed lovers*
> *pining for a paddle-full*
> *of pink-lit solage.*
> *Oh my darling.* Mon cheri!
> *So* bilingues, *so* sophistiqués,
> *as we slip across Confusion Square*
> *to toast our Birken-toes*
> *at the eternally gassy flame…*

By now I'm getting a laugh for every bad pun and bit of fake French. I wiggle my toes in my own happy Birkenstocks. This must be what it feels like to be a stand-up comic, riding on waves of laughter, tracking every reaction. Quite a different feel from reading the poems I usually write, which are carved first for the page. In the kind of performance poetry I'm doing today, the voice and presentation are as much a part of the package as the words themselves.

> *So Sunday slips away*
> *into a humidex August night,*
> *as back between bland sheets,*
> *fingers lightly clasped*
> *(too hot for anything more)*
> *in our riverside* huis clos,
> *we dream ourselves into…*

> *An Ottawa Day!*

I take a breath, to wind myself up to present the frantic, pressured whirr that, in spite of their apparent Ottawa cool, rules the lives of many who work for the politicians and multi-armed bureaucracy, and who leap into the day with –

> *...a 20-minute jog and weights at the RA, then back to well-pressed shirts, the brief-case, where's my lunch?, put out the recycling, can I take the car today? Buzz and whirr, clack and chat, zap those emails, stack that stack of memos, papers, faxes, calls, timely, urgent, zip those halls on ball-bearing toes, files tagged and ready, ADM's briefing notes, press-scrum heady, seven already? Gawd, gotta go, quick pick-ups to make, at the cleaners, the bank machine, stop by Pretoria for the LCBO, back to slogging on the laptop to the tune of "West Wing", then a tray of Loblaw's sushi and a slug of Pelée white, before...*

Whew, I'm out of breath, as I head into the last sixty seconds.

> *Worn to the nub, we turn the heat-exchanger*
> *down another notch, and drop onto the duvet, for...*

> *Ah – love?*
> *After an Ottawa Day?*

This is where the first stanza gets tamed into Ottawa respectability.

> *Oh dear, sex – Ottawa-style.*
> *Round-bellied, hump-shouldered,*
> *sweaty-palmed slick-talker –*

> *and talker, and talker –*

I enjoyed writing this poem, knowing it would give me lots of scope for my inner ham.

Oh, fumbling speech-maker
who keeps memo-ing me back
with your all-too-loose promises,
your snob-nosy bureaucracy,
your must-file cocoon…

But this is Paris on the Rideau. Even in Ottawa sometimes –

though we're bounded by the Eagle,
taxed Air Miles high…

Surely there's lovely love,
Somewhere in Ottawa, love.

Ah, where can we find
in this government town
bilingual intercourse?

I peer around the room.

We're lost in Ottawa, love!
Grumpy, shared sigh….

There's a lot to be said for uninhibited whoops. I trot off the stage, sweating and laughing, to enjoy Oni the Haitian Sensation, with her energetic, sexy delivery and entertaining words.

Last up is Matt Peake; he looks about seventeen. As he rises to read, he thanks his friends from Canterbury (the arts high school) for coming out to support him in such large numbers. (Now how can I complain about that?) Matt's poem is about his love for his brother, who committed suicide this past year. It's passionate and intense, but also well put together. The whole room sighs, as he sits down. Matt wins the audience vote.

And I win a fine memory, and a lighthearted poem, which is played on radio in the next week and brings me many responses. Lovely Ottawa!

The Gargoyle's Left Ear

In January 2003, I again read on Parliament Hill, this time to thousands, and by accident not plan.

"United States Declares War on Iraq"
Winter news. Deep, frozen. Of course the war was coming. It's been coming for months now, but even so I'm seized with anger, and fear for what's to come.

I've left the Gallery early today. Dispirited, hopeless and aimless as the grisly January sky. The traffic is as thick as always on the circle around the peace monument – statues wearing uniforms on a fake crumbling, war-battered wall. What kind of peace does that represent? A snarl of cars stops my progress, as the war seems to have stopped my thoughts. But wait, there's a space behind that truck. I slip through, and head south on Mackenzie, then turn west towards Parliament Hill – it's all I can imagine to do. A few people I vaguely know, peace activists, Quakers, Raging Grannies, artists, writers, politicians – have sent out a joint email to say that if the war starts, gather on the Hill. So that's where I'm going, neck double-wrapped against the wind that spikes around the corners of the new American embassy – that heavily defended cross between a fortress and a battleship – and knifes over Major's Hill Park. My boots slip on the encrusted snow under my feet.

The Château Laurier has its stony back hunched against me, no windows yet lit. I enter through the parking lot for a few warm minutes inside before it's out into the cold again on Wellington Street. All uphill, this trek, and whipped by a north wind. For all the whimsy of the East Tower, which turns two eyes and a nose and a surprised "o" of a mouth to the road, for all the flowers and vines of the cast-iron fences and the glow of the Centennial flame ahead, hissing and burping through a pool ringed with ice, it's just plain cold!

There are more Mounties than usual as I turn onto the Hill, but no-one tries to stop me. The gates are open as always. A straggle of muffled figures trudges heavily, like me, up the main walk towards the Peace Tower. Already there seem to be several thousand people.

I think of the slit windows and blank armoured walls of the American Embassy, of the men with guns standing just inside. This is the second war I've known as an adult that the United States has started and wanted Canada to join. In my bag is a printout of *100 Poets against the War*, gathered on the internet in just one month by Canadian poet Todd Swift. My poem, written two weeks ago, is in there. The anthology has attracted thousands of submissions and will soon be published by Salt, Australia. A similar volume will appear from a British publisher later this month. Another internet project has gathered 10,000 peace poems just this week. There's been lots of publicity. None of it has stopped the war.

The crowd now is too thick for me to see over heads. Every face looks tense; few people are talking. They're listening instead, to a changing procession of speakers on a rough plywood platform built over the stairs that lead to the foot of the Peace Tower. This is the usual venue for events on the Hill, and the expected floodlights are mounted on tripods at each side. Speakers and microphones and reporters and cameras throng the platform and surrounding steps.

More people keep arriving. I'm circling around the edge of the crowd now, over snowbanks piled beside what are large green lawns banked with crocuses each spring. The fragments of conversation I hear ring with grief and anger, but not defeat. We haven't joined the war yet, maybe the Prime Minister can be persuaded to hold out. The Peace Tower looms overhead, so much larger than it appears from Wellington. So gothic, so fanciful in our practical hard land. And yet it's alive with all the words that have been spoken and shouted on these steps that lead to its feet. The gargoyles that are its eyes and ears seem to bend down to listen.

Closer, I can hear better with no distorting boom. It is a widely varied range of community voices coming to the microphone, from unions to politicians to activists to artists. Some shout and thump. Others talk firmly of hope. The Raging Grannies sing.

Suddenly I realise that my poem in the anthology in my bag includes the line, "reading this poem on Parliament Hill." Here I am. How can I ignore this?

"Oops, excuse me."

It's characteristic of Ottawa that no-one tries to stop me as I sidle gingerly up the side steps to the platform, and that, once here, I can introduce myself to one organizer, who finds another, who finds another. Steven Artelle is introducing the speakers. We've never met but it turns out he's heard my name.

"I promise I'll use no more than thirty seconds. What I want isn't exposure for myself but a chance to represent the 10,000 and more poets world-wide who have contributed to peace publications in the weeks just before this. I have the first printout of an anthology –"

"Is that *100 Poets against the War*? Yes, I've seen it on the internet. I think we could just slip you in after this speaker if you keep it really short."

Steven steps in front of politician Jack Layton.

"We have one poem to do first, if you don't mind." Jack steps back.

"I'm here to represent 10,000 poets..."

The microphone booms, the faces look up.

Against the war I'll refuse
to be insulted today.
Against the war I'll recite this poem
on Parliament Hill,
drive my car not at all,
gossip about love...

I'm reading to thousands of people, more than ever before, but it's not about me and I'm surprised to find that my voice is steady.

Against the war I'll act
today, as I can, for peace

Jack Layton nods at me, and steps forward into my place. On this bitter winter evening, I wonder if anyone beyond this gathering is listening to any of us.

Jack Layton went on to succeed Alexa McDonough as leader of the New Democratic Party. She gave *Convergence* a warm, even moving, reception. Eighteen months after the event on the Hill, he walked alone and down these same steps on a fall day to accept a poem and book from me as part of the national project, "Random

Acts of Poetry." Did he remember me, is that why he came? I was too flustered to ask. But I did notice that the poem he chose for me to read is a poem about being too often away from the one you love. And that he listens well. MPs Ed Broadbent and Herb Gray also met me and Ronnie Brown for Random Acts, as did city councillor (and Quaker) Clive Doucet, actor Paul Gross, and dozens of others, including my friends Charlie, Levi, Gail, and Ross at the R.A. Centre where I go to exercise (I ran out of books there, should have brought more).

And it turns out that Jean Chrétien, at least, did listen to those many Canadians who were on Parliament Hill on that black, January day in 2003, urging the government to stay out of Iraq. Chrétien may even have heard me read the poem, and noticed that it came from a Canadian anthology.

And he may have remembered receiving a peace poem three years before. According to Sandra Stephenson, writing for Sam Hamill's *Poets against War* internet newsletter in fall 2006, "It could be that a contingent of 52 poets under the name 'Convergence,' who hand-delivered peace poems wrapped in original art to Ottawa Parliamentarians in 2001, who held a reading at the National Arts Centre four days after September 11, swayed the vote that kept Canada out of Iraq at a time when public opinion polls claimed that Canadians favoured war." Whatever the reason, the Prime Minister and the Parliament of February 2003 refused to join the war against Iraq. I forget many things, but I won't forget that.

Until the Light Bends

In the fall of 2003, I took the unwieldy "Rideau Falls" poem I'd written in 1988 for bpNichol to a poetry colloquium at Sage Hill, led by Fred Wah, also a friend of bp's and, like him, an explorer. He suggested introducing a mysterious "it" that would distance the poem and let it turn on an axis of rhythm. I'd already placed the work within a larger cycle of death poems that I was moulding from their very individual and specific beginnings into a fictionalized, single story of loss.

*Fred's strategy worked. The fourteen-poem cycle, now called "Ordinary," became the central element in my next poetry book, **Until the Light Bends**, published by Marty Gervais of Black Moss Press in July 2004.*

Some months before the book came out, Sheila Ross and Scot Dunlop of Wolf Moon asked us to join them for a concert in March 2004 sponsored by the Ottawa Folk Festival – my fourth time at the Fourth Stage. By now, Geode was a changing mix of three to seven musicians, with Alrick and me at the core. We asked the six musicians who would come to the NAC to each take a poem or more from the new book and prepare a musical environment for it, anything from a few suggestions to a complete notation. The CD eventually issued to match the book shows that Alrick prepared "Sleet" and "How God Sees," Jennifer Giles took on "Sonata for Watcher and Shades," Jamie Gullikson did "Starlings," John Higney prepared "Still," Mark Molnar set "Ice," and David Broscoe composed a setting for "Ordinary."

We're taping this gig. We've spent all afternoon doing sound checks, we've spent a month promoting the show, we've spent six months writing the music and rehearsing, the space is perfect for us, perfect in size and setup, with technicians and ushers and a green room and a bar and café tables arranged in a friendly arc around the plain black stage. The instruments glow with a soft brass and gold and ebony and mahogany sheen under the lights: Jen's grand piano upstage right, John's guitars and Mark's violin and cello downstage of her, my mic in the middle, Dave's sax and bassoon and clarinet downstage right, Jamie's collection of percussion and drums glittering behind him, Alrick's bass upstage centre. A small stage for so many, but tight, intimate, embracing.

Chris White from the Ottawa Folk Festival completes his introduction, I stride the last few steps to the stage, lift my foot – and the lights go out. Black, totally black. The heel of my new shoes catches on the edge and flings me forward stiff and fast as a dropped two-by-four. The lights flash up on flying music and stands and instruments as I go down, twisting sideways in the last split second to avoid landing all my weight on the cello that crashes beside me. *The cello's worth more than I am!* I think in panic, and freeze. Alrick's bass is just behind my head.

"I caught it, it's okay!" Missy's voice, I don't dare look.

"Are you all right? Don't move." A kind woman bends over me. She looks familiar but I'm too shaken to make a connection.

I try to ignore a balloon of hysteria rising in my throat. She pulls me carefully to my feet; there's another pair of hands behind my shoulders.

"The bass is fine," Alrick whispers as he shuffles papers back onto his stand. Missy, friend and singer, crossed behind the stage to get to her seat at the crucial moment.

John looks up from checking his lap steel. "You missed me," he grins.

Dave lifts his clarinet to his lips, one hand smoothing pages. Eyebrows raise over concerned eyes.

I nod at him – it's all right, I'm okay – and turn to Jennifer, who beams at me from the piano, strong as a stage light.

Jamie runs a quick shuffle across his drum and leans forward, brushes poised.

And Mark. Mark is passing his cello to a friend at one of the tables offstage.

"Is it broken? Oh no!" I'm trying to whisper to him, but my throat is hoarse.

"It's okay, I'll play my violin. It's okay!" Mark mouths back at me.

My heart still thuds. He looks at me, smiles.

I take a deep breath. Step up onto the stage. Carefully. Adjust the mic and stand. Set my legs under me. They will not tremble!

Look out at the audience. There are two choices: burst into tears, or start the show.

"Well. That was quite an entrance!"

A small laugh from a few throats. A shadowed crowd, waiting, all looking at me.

Glance from musician to musician, around the circle. Waiting. Looking at me. Ready.

Mark lifts his bow, grins. I throw back my shoulders and raise my chin, half turn to the bass.

Dum-dah-dahdahdahdah, dum-dah-dahdahdahdah. The drum picks up, clarinet and guitar ease in, piano enters rhythmic and strong, violin slips a sly line under my words as we begin a spoof called *Bitter Bread*.

You prepare a feast of bitter bread,
of acid wine and rancid flesh...

I make devil eyes at the audience, turn from face to face to catch a twinkle, pull out a grin. They're with me, the band, too. It's hooting and pounding and whipping round the notes round the circle.

...and the bread that is thrust
on one who has erred
in matters of love
must always be –

– hold, hold – all together –

shared!

A hundred clapping hands. We're launched.

The next hour passes in a golden haze. The players weave a net of sound and light that sparkles like a lake whipped by spring wind. I toss my words into it, onto it, under it, we riff and play and the audience leaps with us, for a dozen poems.

And then I still my hands and eyes and gather them all in, listeners and players, sound and light people, bartender and ushers, and ask them to follow as we dive into a half-hour long lament for lost life and love.

The clarinet lays out a clear, soft line. The violin adds a whisper below. Bit by bit, the piano and steel guitar and bass join in.

– ordinary – is it?
as bread
or the taste of water
        it is?

As we count the measures through fourteen sections, each instrument plays out its unique solos, and twos and threes and fours join in swaths of colour and melody, the seven of us lifting together at times into a harmony so loose and yet close that we've never come near it before.

how
    the window jewels
        crocuses, rich
            purple, blue on rags of snow

In a brief moment when the band is soaring into a long slow swell I think how great it is that we arranged to tape this show that is, even though I fell – or maybe because I fell – the best we've done.

The music breaks apart into strands that curve down to a breath …

She lies so still I can hardly tell
if she's here or gone…

Then the violin arcs, alone, into the space, carrying my voice with it into another realm. This is why I bring my words to musicians and work with them, for the tapestries the sounds and words make together, richer than either on its own.

We can only endure it.
The dread, the sweats…

In the moments when silence falls briefly, there's not a rustle or breath from the audience. Every ear is open at the last as –

…blasted
with spray it
pounds
it
drenches
it
will not
stop
I can
not turn
away from
it
she
falls and
          falls
               – mouth full
                    of roar –

A crash of percussion.
Out of the dark the tenor sax sends a single clear call.

… is it, *after all,*
ordinary –

The violin adds a rising note, the steel guitar offers echos and bells, the piano ripples through the rush of drum and lullaby of bass –

The sky
shifts grey
to red
to green –

by my foot
is a pool of
water –
it shines –

Afterwards, in the midst of the comments and congratulations and laughter and relief, and sadness too, for those who aren't here, I'm glad to be able to tell everyone who asks that yes, there is a recording of the show, and yes, I'll let everyone know, and yes it was the best we've ever done, and yes we'll get the cello fixed and yes and yes and yes...

In the second half, Sheila Ross and Scott Dunlop of Wolf Moon present their entrancing poetry and music to warm applause. The evening is declared a great success.

As we pack to leave, the sound man comes over. You did a terrific job balancing the voice and instruments, I tell him. It's a show I'll never forget and I'm so glad we caught it on tape.

Well, as for that. He shuffles, winces. Looks up at me, then down. I forgot to turn on the recorder, he says. I rode the levels and everything, but I forgot to turn on the machine.

And so I can tell you, for certain, that, on that evening at the National Arts Centre, we soared, we flew, as we never have before or since, that the audience was transported. That this was the best performance Geode has ever done. Because who can prove me wrong?

We did, in the end, record those pieces six months later, at James Stephens' Stove Studio in Chelsea, Québec, and it became the CD *Until the Light Bends* produced by Penn Kemp and Gavin Stairs of Pendas Productions in 2004. (James also helped record *SugarBeat* in 1998, and *Geode* in 2000.) The end result is different than the Fourth Stage show. For one thing, Mark had his cello back, better than before, he said. But it was still as hard to perform, still as all-engulfing. We could only do so many sectional retakes. At the end we were exhausted. And I was, for a while, beyond words.

Amazing Grace

Above all, it's a good harmony song. How many times have we ended our sing-songs at the lake with a twelve- or fifteen-voice rendition, all of us on our feet, all improvising our own parts, with an effect that, echoing across the moon-mirroring lake, is glorious to our ears.

And it's a good title. The words of the verses are old-fashioned bible-thumpers that roll around in the mouth but mean little to any of us personally. The title, on the other hand – well yes, it is amazing, this gathering of community, and yes, what is it but grace, this happiness, unexpected, unearned?

"The Gargoyle's Left Ear." Is that a good title? And why is the title almost always the last thing to be written?

I sit back with a sigh, put down my pen, stretch my hand. I was hoping to finish the book this weekend, but the solar panel's on the fritz, and I'm writing in longhand. A manuscript, not a typescript. It's been a long time since I sat here like this with nothing but a pen in my hand and a yellow pad of lined paper and the loons whooping and quarrelling in the dusk.

And it's a rare weekend indeed that I sit at the cottage table alone. A bowl of cottage cheese and pot of twig tea replace the feasts we've held here of coq au vin, roast pork and apples, whole fresh trout taken from the lake that morning, though admittedly asparagus and new potatoes and raspberries await my mother's arrival this afternoon. It's impossible not to bring at least a few treats to the cottage.

It's even harder to get away from people, here, than from food. A chorus of *rack-rack-ack* draws my eyes up from the page and out through the window to the glitter of wind fret on the water. The family of merganser ducks that circle the lake twice a day have stopped as usual just beyond our rock where the fishing for small new bass is excellent.

The ducks are the only neighbours I see this Friday evening, but I can hear voices from across the bay, and more from up the hill. When we bought our place in 1980, Pete and Colleen Martin came to visit, and took a tour around the lake. Two weeks later, they paddled past us in a new bright yellow canoe as we sat on the beach eating supper. They'd just purchased the cottage two lots over, across Turtle Bay from John Tappin.

John is up this weekend too, fishing, leaving Marie at home huddled over her computer. Now I've discovered one solar panel will run a laptop, maybe she'll spend more time at the lake. He'll drop by later, for a glass of wine, and my niece Margaret, who's been staying with my mother at her cottage nearby, will stop in for tea before heading back to Ottawa. It's surprising, in the constant press of people and events at the lake, that so much of my writing has started here. Perhaps it's the silence, an underlying silence made of thrush call and mouse rustle, of wave lap and wind rush and rain patter, all offering paths to thought. Perhaps it's the clear air and dark nights – a plunging deep darkness made of star spatter on the black glass lake, moon pour through uncurtained windows, aurora alive over the opposite shore. The darkness slides me into ten or more hours of solid sleep every night, so I awake with words in my hand.

Even the parade of people passing through carries its own brand of silence, a silence of removal from urban clamour. Each one is family or friend, so there's no need for social masks. And they talk to me not through a distance buzz of phone or email or text-message, but face to face, and about immediate things. "What's for supper?" "Want to come for a swim?" Their arrival requires no more from me than a move from kitchen table to couch or porch, with a stop at the fridge in passing. When we do talk at length, it's in a story-telling, philosophical ramble that sprinkles more poem ideas along the way, instead of drowning them in noise.

I put another log on the fire, a piece of the yellow birch Ian cut in the woods last fall and dried on the porch all winter. I'm still not sure about the air-tight wood stove we put in last year. It smokes, and doesn't heat as quickly as the conical Acorn we used to have. This cottage is suspicious of change.

Because nothing much changes here. Even in the dim light I can see the paddles decorated by my mother with a cutout red carp and our family motto, "carpe diem," hanging on the walls, near the grass basket made by Jean Gubby and the rainbow carp painting from my aunt Jean, the dream catcher from Arlette and Steve, and the cornucopia woven by Morel and Roberta one year for the annual Thanksgiving feast at the Martins. Their small dark cottage has been transformed over the years to accommodate their quickly growing circle of family and friends, with sleeping wing and bunkie, bathroom with hot water, and full wrap-around porch, much of it built by Bill Morgan. Bill was making maple syrup in his sugar shack, when he had a fatal heart attack, not the worst way to go.

Bill also built my mother's Cadillac outhouse, as well as the outhouse for Gwen and Steve's cottage next door. In turn, these gave rise to a poem of mine entitled "Outhouse," which is posted in a number of privies around the lake and elsewhere, raising the question of what place, exactly, people have for poetry in their lives.

No question about the place of music. So many voices for so many sing-songs on our beach and before our fire, songs made up on the spot and dredged up from memory and books and written down in little chapbooks and handed around at every gathering.

When they were young, Coff entranced the kids – his and Gwen's children Meredith and Gaelan, plus our two, and others like Kyla and Haley and Stephanie and Ron and Tim, if they turned up, with wonderful funny tales made up on the spot. I wish we'd written them down.

All our siblings have visited at some time, as well. Martha and Vince and Vivien and Sandy brought new voices and songs into the circle. Jeremiah and Sam each came for solo visits, and then Ann and Hugh and Becca joined them another year and helped roof our porch. Peter made a special visit from Alberta, and Mary and Mike drop by from time to time. Ian's brother and sister have each left contributions – stones set well in the path from Alison, and a whimsical driftwood manikin from Jim.

The younger crew seldom get here anymore from their hectic lives in Montreal and Calgary and Sudbury. But the new generation has two members to date – our great nephew Jake and our grandchild Eric – so I hope it won't be long before the cycle of large noisy family gatherings starts again.

So many people. I can't possibly list them all. As I sit here in solitude, toes slowly chilling against the plywood floor, they parade before me, a horde, a host, of faces. Patrick and John McMaster splitting wood for frigid New Years' celebrations, Aven and Mark and Morel and Ian clearing a strip of ice for "body-curling" while I laugh and nurse my back, Alrick playing bass to the loons, Nancy and Eric in deck chairs on the sand with their books and hats, Nathan holding up a fish bigger than his father's, Solomon painting a picture on the outhouse wall of his mom canoeing, Andrew climbing down the cliff after arriving from Pembroke by taxi, Mark's parents Shiv and Danielle and his aunt Mythily at ease on the screened-in porch, Anne and Gordon skinny dipping, unconcerned about binoculars, birthday parties for everyone at once, because this is where we meet...

Stories captured only in bits, in occasional "cottage journal" entries and numerous photos, undated, uninscribed.

We thought we would remember.

And yet, as I glance around at items from times and people long past, I wonder how important it is to track and replay all the elements of our lives. Every person, every life, is a full container of stories untold. Untold, but not un-enjoyed. Why not just sit here, quietly, and let the ghosts drift past, and maybe, if the time is right, pluck a poem from the pageant?

The stove has stopped smoking, and the fire is finally blazing. Maybe all it needed was patience.

Poetry books and recordings by Susan McMaster

Until the Light Bends (Black Moss, 2004, CD Pendas, 2004)
Uncommon Prayer: A Book of Dedications (Quarry, 1997)
Learning to Ride (Quarry, illus. Robert Verrall, 1994)
The Hummingbird Murders (Quarry, 1992)
Dark Galaxies (Ouroboros, 1986)
North/South (Underwhich, w. A. McClure, C. Morton, 1986)
Pass this way again (Underwhich, w. A. McClure, C. Dupuis,1983)
GEODE Music & Poetry (CD, 2000)
SugarBeat Music & Poetry (CD, 1998)
Wordmusic (audiotape, 1986)
La Deriva del Pianeta, trans./ed. Ada Donati (Schifanoia, 2003)
Waging Peace: Poetry and Political Action, ed. (Penumbra, 2002)
Convergence: Poets for Peace, ed. (League of Canadian Poets, boxed sets, plus poems with art, 2001, CD, 2002)
Siolence: Poets on Women, Violence and Silence, ed. (Quarry, 1998)
Bookware: Ottawa Valley Poets, co-ed. w. C. Morton (LCP, 1994)
Dangerous Graces: Women's Poetry on Stage, ed./script (Balmuir, 1987)
Branching Out Magazine, founding ed., 1973–75, contrib. 1975–80
Vernissage: the Magazine of the National Gallery of Canada, founding ed.-in-chief, 1999–2001

Lines quoted in the text are unpublished or come from the above publications. "Civil Service" appears in *A Discord of Flags*, Steven Heighton, ed. (1991). Also see web.ncf.ca/smcmaster